The
Year
of the
Poet X

December 2023

The Poetry Posse

inner child press, ltd.

The Poetry Posse 2023

Gail Weston Shazor

Shareef Abdur Rasheed

Teresa E. Gallion

hülya n. yılmaz

Kimberly Burnham

Tzemin Ition Tsai

Elizabeth Esguerra Castillo

Jackie Davis Allen

Joe Paire

Caroline 'Ceri' Nazareno

Ashok K. Bhargava

Alicja Maria Kuberska

Swapna Behera

Albert 'Infinite' Carrasco

Michelle Joan Barulich

Eliza Segiet

William S. Peters, Sr.

~ * ~

In order to maintain each poet's authentic voice, this volume has not undergone the scrutiny of editing. Please take time to indulge each contributor for their own creativity and aspirations to convey their uniqueness.

hülya n. yılmaz, Ph.D.
Director of Editing ~
Inner Child Press International

General Information

The Year of the Poet X
December 2023 Edition

The Poetry Posse

1st Edition : 2023

Publisher Information
1st Edition : Inner Child Press
intouch@innerchildpress.com
www.innerchildpress.com

Copyright © 2023 : The Poetry Posse

ISBN-13 : 978-1-961498-12-9 (inner child press, ltd.)

$ 12.99

WHAT WOULD LIFE BE WITHOUT A LITTLE POETRY?

Dedication

This Book is dedicated to

Humanity, Peace & Poetry

the Power of the Pen

can effectuate change!

&

The Poetry Posse

past, present & future,

our Patrons and Readers &

the Spirit of our Everlasting Muse

In the darkness of my life
I heard the music
I danced . . .
and the Light appeared
and I dance

Janet P. Caldwell

Table of Contents

The Poetry Posse

Table of Contents . . . *continued*

December's Featured Poets   111

Inner Child Press News   143

Other Anthological Works   181

Foreword
Children: Difference Makers

Melati and Isabel Wijsen

As I write down these words, children are being killed by war mongers in several parts of the world *yet once again*. The lives of our most precious are being cut abruptly and violently *yet once again*, only to count as numbers of "fatalities"—if at all. It is a no-brainer to imagine that some of those children could have become notable enough to be honored for their groundbreaking inventions, discoveries or services to humanity at large, had they been allowed to live the natural course of their times on Earth. Not unlike the focus of the issue in your hands—Melati and Isabel Wijsen.

For the entire year of 2023, our monthly book's Poetry Posse and all featured poets had their eyes on children who made a difference on and to our planet. While calling attention to the humanitarian services of Melati Wijsen and Isabel Wijsen in 2023's final month, I cannot help but view the bigger picture: What if these Indonesian sisters, 10- and 12-years old respectively when they attained the consciousness to raise a much-needed awareness among their fellow humans, were born into one of our modern-day war-torn countries? What if one of the siblings or both then became "a casualty" in that world region? Two remarkably influential children, who made a difference of consequence in and for our earthly plane, would have been dismissed, or better yet, discarded at the same speed and with the same indifference as all the children killed in wars in so-called modern times.

The UN Committee on the Rights of the Child recently reported its ongoing data, stating that one out of every five children worldwide live within armed conflict zones. A total of 2,985 children were killed across 24 countries in 2022, 2,515 in 2021, 2,674 in 2020 across 22 countries, and 4,019 children in 2019—according to the last three Annual Reports of the UN Secretary-General on Children and Armed Conflict. How many of those who are anon counted among the dead could have or would have become significant contributors to our humanity's needs and for its development?

So, as we through our poems celebrate the achievements of two sisters from Bali, I am reminded of the horrendous realities of all the children who presently are bound to those world zones where there is an armed conflict. We can only hope, as I desperately want to, that children in the likes of the Bali-natives Melati and Isabel Wijsen from Indonesia would one day survive the mindset of warmongering before it is birthed.

hülya n. yılmaz, Ph.D.

Penn State Professor Emerita, Liberal Arts
Director of Editing Services, Inner Child Press International

Coming April 2024

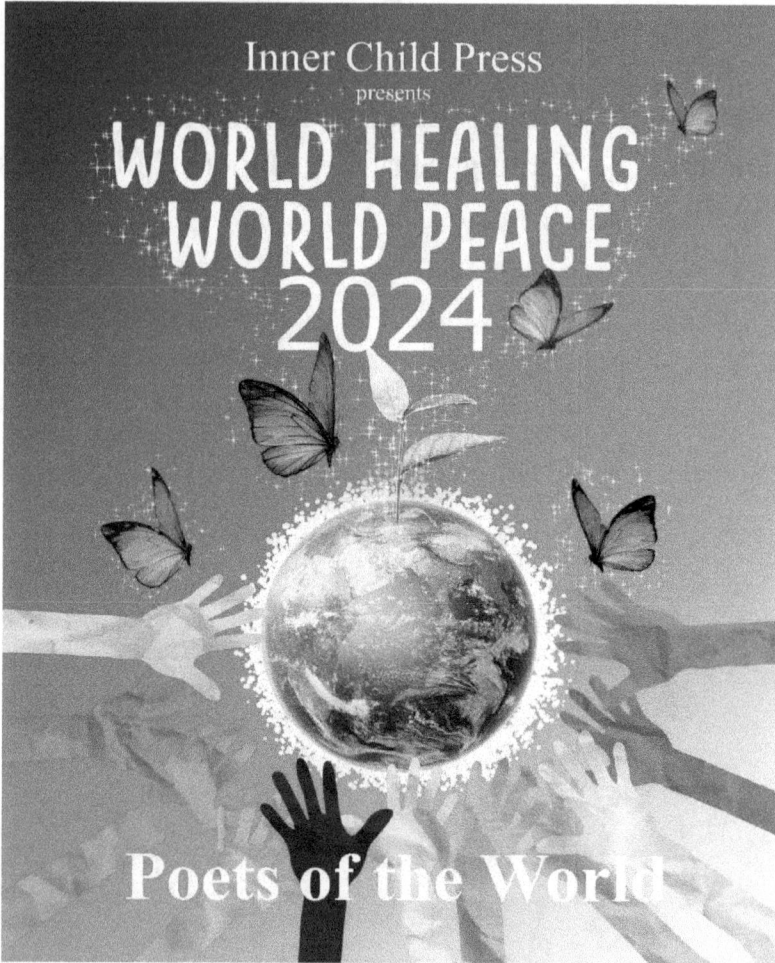

Inner Child Press
presents

WORLD HEALING
WORLD PEACE
2024

Poets of the World

www.innerchildpress.com/world-healing-
world-peace-poetry

Preface

We, **Inner Child Press International, The Year of the Poet** and **The Poetry Posse** welcome you.

WOW . . . a decade. We are so excited as we are now offer unto you our final month of our **10th** year of monthly publication of this enterprise, **The Year of the Poet**.

This particular year we have chosen to feature children who made/make a difference in enhancing the lives of all humanity. Read ~ Learn.

For those of you who are not familiar with our story, back in 2013, a few of us poets got together with the simple intention of producing a book a month. That was our challenge. Since that time the enterprise has blossomed and brought forth a fruit that seems to keep on growing as evidenced as we enter 2023.

Our purpose is simple. Through our lyrical words and verse, we not only wish to share our poetic works, but we also have the poetic naiveté to believe that we can assist in the growth of consciousness of the things that have an effect our collective humanity. Therefore, we welcome your readership. For more about what we are attempting to accomplish, have a look at our Publishing Web Site . . . www.innerchildpress.com. If you would like to

know a bit more about this particular endeavor please stop by for a visit at :
www.innerchildpress.com/the-year-of-the-poet

Over the years, Inner Child Press has been socially active to bring awareness and catalog through literature the things that have an impact upon our world and its inhabitants. We have solicited, produced, underwritten and published quite a few volumes to that end. For more insight you may wish to visit : www.innerchildpress.com/the-anthology-market. If you are a writer, poet, or activist, you would be advised to keep a eye out for upcoming volumes should you desire to participate. All readers are welcomed as well. Note, that there is a myriad of published volumes that are available as a FREE PDF download as well as available for purchase at affordable prices.

We at this time extend to you our well wishes for your own personal journey and hope that you consider including us as a travel companion.

Bless Up

Bill

William S. Peters, Sr.

Publisher
Inner Child Press International
www.innerchildpress.com

Children

Difference Makers

Melati and Isabel Wijsen

December 2023

by Kimberly Burnham, Ph.D.

Melati and Isabel Wijsen were only 10 and 12, respectively, when they started on a course of activism that has drastically decreased the global usage of single-use plastic. The young women were inspired by the country of Rwanda's ban of polyethylene bags in 2008 and decided to try to get their native Bali to do the same. Their homegrown initiative of beach cleanups and government petitions graduated to an organization advocating for reduced plastic use in 15 different countries. Bali is officially plastic bag free, and Indonesia will be by 2021, with the Wijsen to thank.

"Find that one thing that you're incredibly passionate about, that you think about 24/7. This is important because focusing on one thing allows you to find that tangible way that you can make a difference." — Melati Wijsen, Founder, Bye Bye Plastic Bags

Poets . . .
sowing seeds in the
Conscious Garden of Life,
that those who have yet to come
may enjoy the Flowers.

Poets, Writers . . . know that we are the enchanting magicians that nourishes the seeds of dreams and thoughts . . . it is our words that entice the hearts and minds of others to believe there is something grand about the possibilities that life has to offer and our words tease it forth into action . . . for you are the Poet, the Writer to whom the Gift of Words has been entrusted . . .

~ wsp

poetry is . . .

Poetry succeeds where instruction fails.

~ wsp

Now Available

Letter Poems
to our
Deceased
featuring
Poets of the World

www.innerchildpress.com/the-anthology-market.com

Gail Weston Shazor

Gail Weston Shazor

Gail Weston Shazor is a lover of words. She is fond of the arcane, unusual and the not yet words.

Coining words at an early age, there was often a bit of trouble with teachers, but she always had her mother and aunt to back up her choices in expression. Born in Mississippi, she spent her early years with her grandparents. Each of the four left very careful influences on her pre-schooling. She learned in turn how women worked in and out of the home and how men worked in and out of the home to support the family. She learned that a lack of proper schooling was not the only way to learn and understanding life was a great teacher. As in most rural families of color, women had a greater chance of formal learning. Both of Gail's grandmothers read out loud to the family whether it was the bible or the newspapers and important documents to their spouses.

Gail Weston Shazor has authored (so far) Notes from the Blue Roof, A Overstanding of an Imperfect Love, HeartSongs and Lies My Grandfather's Told Me. The number of anthologies is too many to list with the premier accomplishment of one of the contributors to The Year of The Poet. Gail will always lend her ink to community projects and will purchase the books of fellow poets in the Inner Child Press family.

Standing in the wilderness shouting

I am here, arms wide open
Waiting on my creator to
Speak
Talk
Move
Give
Me something for you
So that I can be obedient
To fall on my knees in fasting
Eating only the words of
Life
Death
Birth
Stillness
With all the power of first
And all the waiting of last
Beginning and end
The words of the crafter
Poet
Writer
Lyricist
Deliverer
And I will ink it quick
Placing it everywhere you are
So that you can see and hear
What is in store for you
Me
They
Us
All
There is never a time

When the word was not offered
Only when it was not received
And not called forth to teach
Truth
Wisdom
Correction
Love
For that is our purpose
And why were made
And what we have been
Ordered to spread among
Ghettos
Cities
Fields
Hearts
Til all has been healed
I remain
Standing in the wilderness shouting

Koinonia

To receive goodness
We must first pour out
All that we have
All that we are
All that they have given us
To make room for the grace
This is the secret
Of living goodness
That the world never shares with us
This is the secret that only family
Can teach us
And even then
Sometimes
Our only heart breaks
In times such as these
It is a hard thing
This living broken
But this, my loves,
Is when the newly formed spaces
Shine brighter than the
Lived through ones
The simple connection
Becomes the necessary
And we have to keep seeking
The strength of each other
And in the broken places
We make room for more
More love
More people
More community
And love is always a sacrifice
And love is always intentional
And living is the love we share
Through all our numbered days
Selah

Poet (slammed)

I listen to your words
Angry, sullen and revolutionary words
You want change
And
You want it now
I hear your words
You scream at the injustice
Of your childhood
Absent father
Drug addicted sister
And you had to eat free lunch at school
I taste your words
Bitter and hungry at the same time
You wound the ear
In tirades
Leaving a trail
Of vowels
Not ink
For that last too long
Establishmentarianism
Which you are against
Form and substance
Eaten and spewed back out
I smell your words
Categorically denied
That you are also tomorrow
For tomorrow brings a new fight
A new struggle
Found deep
In your recycled bag
Of hemp and straw and lies
Green

Reclaimed
You rally for the latest buzz
I feel your words
Tight and hot
Quick and sharp words
Thorns on rose bushes unseen
Bleeding out the ones without knowledge
And then you leave for the next
March, next stage
In your gas guzzling SUV
Starbuck coffee in hand
A "spoken word" artist
And over your shoulder
You loudly accuse me of being
A "poet".

Alicja Maria Kuberska

Alicja Maria Kuberska – awarded Polish poetess, novelist, journalist, editor.

She is a member of the Polish Writers Associations in Warsaw, Poland and IWA Bogdani, Albania. She is also a member of directors' board of Soflay Literature Foundation, Our Poetry Archive (India) and Cultural Ambassador for Poland (Inner Child Press, USA)

Her poems have been published in numerous anthologies and magazines in : Poland, Czech Republic, Slovakia, Hungary,Ukraina, Belgium, Bulgaria, Albania, Spain, the UK, Italy, the USA, Canada, the UK, Argentina, Chile, Peru, Israel, Turkey, India, Uzbekistan, South Korea, Taiwan, China, Australia, South Africa, Zambia, Nigeria

She received two medals - the Nosside UNESCO Competition in Italy (2015) and European Academy of Science Arts and Letters in France (2017). Ahe also received a reward of international literary competition in Italy ,, Tra le parole e 'elfinito" (2018). She was announced a poet of the 2017 year by Soflay Literature Foundation (2018).She also received : Bolesław Prus Prize Poland (2019), Culture Animator Poland (2019) and first prize Premio Internazionale di Poesia Poseidonia- Paestrum Italy (2019).

Plastic bags

They fell like autumn leaves
on river waters and soil.
They drift in the seas and oceans

Eternally white,
almost immortal,
they are not subject
to the cycles of nature

The leaves of the trees will rot
and they will crumble to dust
Plastic will last forever.

They were supposed
to be a godsend,
replace paper
to protect the trees.

They have become a curse
and seeped in everywhere.
They are suffocating the planet.

Rain

Drops glitter on the spider's web
- it's rain caught in a net,
stretched between
heaven and earth.

The particles glisten with silver
and shine like white opals.
They sparkle with rainbow colours

It is a pity, drops will soon disappear.
They will rise to the clouds,
to touch existence.

Night Dreads

On a starless night
the wind sings differently.
The leaves shake with anxiety,
the branches are bent by fear.

Owls hoot,
wake up the dark hours.
The blackness of the clouds
falls soundlessly to dreams.

Don't wake me up now.
Let the sun rise
and tickle with a ray.
I am a child of light.

I don't want to be afraid.

Jackie

Davis

Allen

Jackie Davis Allen, otherwise known as Jacqueline D. Allen or Jackie Allen, grew up in the Cumberland Mountains of Appalachia. As the next eldest daughter of a coal miner father and a stay at home mother, she was the first in her family to attend and graduate from college. Her siblings, in their own right, are accomplished, though she is the only one, to date, that has discovered the gift of writing.

Graduating from Radford University, with a Bachelor's of Science degree in Early Education, she taught in both public and private schools. For over a decade she taught private art classes to children both in her home and at a local Art and Framing Shop where she also sold her original soft sculptured Victorian dolls and original christening gowns.

She resides in northern Virginia with her husband, taking much needed get-aways to their mountain home near the Blue Ridge Mountains, a place that evokes memories of days spent growing up in the Appalachian Mountains.

A lover of hats, she has worn many. Following marriage to her college sweetheart, and as wife, mother, grandmother, teacher, tutor, artist, writer, poet and crafter, she is a lover of art and antiques, surrounding herself, always, with books, seeking to learn more.

In 2015 she authored *Looking for Rainbows, Poetry, Prose and Art*, and in 2017, *Dark Side of the Moon*. Both books of mostly narrative poetry were published by Inner Child Press and were edited by hulya n. yilmaz in 2019, *No Illusions. Through the Looking Glass*, which was nominated to be considered for a Pulitzer Prize by the publisher and editor of Inner Child Press, ltd.

http://www.innerchildpress.com/jackie-davis-allen.php
jackiedavisallen.com

Making a Difference

Melati and Isabel Wijsen, two sisters, at the age of 10 and 12, convinced their country, Bali, to ban the use of single-use plastic.

"Once upon a time",
So the Fairy Tales begin,
But, let me assure you,
This is no Fairy Tale.

From the efforts, of two young sisters
Inspired by concern's commitment,
Decided to do something.
And, they were successful!

Inspired by Rwanda's 2008 success
Of banning single use plastic bags,
Today, thankfully, Bali is also
Free of the same. Thanks to Melati and Isabel.

Is there not something that can be
Learned from these two young girls?
Something that you can do, no matter
How small, to make a difference?

Something Happened

Whatever happened, happened.
And though each wished it had not, it did.
And great was the pain that came.
With time, supplication, prayers, shall sorrow not
Be replaced by love's intentional action?

It never should have happened, yet it did.

Was there anything either could have done?
Could either have prevented, changed the perception
Of the other's actions? Or the words that brought
On the blame and shame
Of those cold winter days?

Alas, it never should have happened.

Threatening skies grew dark
While the sleet and hail of words
Screamed alienation.
Wallowing in self pity, pride's suffering
Mended not their wounds.

Lo, the price paid for forgetting the Golden Rule.

Hear Me, O Lord

I've come, bruised and empty,
Searching for that which once quenched my thirst,
Longing to be relieved of the emptiness
That consumes my every thought.

I am crying, mourning the loss
Of my creative voice.

Yielded up and waiting,
I silently mouth the words,
Praying that once again the poetic waters may flow,
Even as I await your perfect Will.

I am determined to stay on bended knee
If that is what it takes.

Why is it that the flowers continue to bloom,
The rains still fall, yet within,
That which once flourished seems wilted,
Dead or dying?

Do you hear me crying?
Father, I am here! Do with me as You please.

What's that?
I wonder if I am dreaming,
Though clearly I hear my name!
"Dearest child, you called out to me.

And I have come, so rise up from self pity,
You whom I have created with so much promise."

I slowly rise, as the Spirit
Continues to counsel me.

"Waiting for me to work a miracle
Is not the answer to your thirst.
Use the gifts I've given you, and in the effort
You'll discover that which you seek.

And you will be satisfied!"
Oh, with such great truth supplied,

I knew my request would not be denied.
Thank you, oh great Creator.
I now understand that the gifts and talents
Within, those that once flourished, must be used.

And, that neglect is not the answer.

Tzemin
Ition
Tsai

Dr. Tzemin Ition Tsai comes from the Republic of China(Taiwan). In addition to being a professor of literature at a university, he is more committed to writing poems, novels, and proses. He is also an editor of "Reading, Writing and Teaching" academic text, an International editor of "Contemporary dialogues" literary periodical in Macedonia, and Vice-Chairman of the International Jury of the SAHITTO INTERNATIONAL AWARD in Bangladesh, and a columnist for "Chinese Language Monthly" in Taiwan.

In a wide range of literary creations, he is particularly fond of interesting stories or novels, and writing articles or poems about the feelings of nature and human beings. He has won many national literary awards. His literary works have been anthologized and published in books, journals, and newspapers in more than 55 countries and have been translated into more than 24 languages.

The Sounds Of The Lane

Within this steel shell,
The iron bridge's copper pillars are spotlessly clean.
Banana leaves and maple leaves,
Gone beyond the ear's reach.
The west wind,
Sneaks in quietly.
In the lane,
The branches of the pomelo tree are ordered to blow down
the wind from the wall.

Under the flowers,
Shadows stretch out in a line.
Are they white branches? Are they green branches?
Are they the spring flowers' windblown branches?
Are they the autumn leaves' blown-away branches?
In the mezzanine,
A timid bookstore.
Modern poems,
Still lonely between the pages.

A low house with a brick wall,
Counting the passing of time.
The hand pump stands alone,
Declaring that the childhood that has passed for fifty years
is beyond recall.
A wild house with a cucumber trellis.
The magical lane,
Freezes time.
Allowing me to steal just half a day,
To live my life as it is.

Wisteria's Secret

I Sealed within this trellis of wisteria,
My heart is warmed by the sun's embrace.
As petals flutter to the ground,
I follow them with my eyes.
The pale lilac hue is both haunting and beautiful,
Like a tongue that licks and devours the falling flowers.
My youth is restless, and I will not let love linger on the
wall outside.
The fireworks are a beautiful sight, drawing me to the east,
like a gentle breeze.
The stream is cold and clear, counting the many words, I
have spoken.
I flaunt my secret, which I will never reveal this.

If not for the scattered leaves,
I would not have seen the lone crow perched in surprise on
the wisteria vine.
March is not yet cool, and the flowers are just about to ask,
Who is the true master of this place?
In April, the grass is lush and the garden is in full bloom.
The colorful vines should not pretend to be willow
branches, but rather reveal their pale green hue.
In the unsanctioned red glow of the evening sun, the spring
breeze gently savors the fragrant scent of spring.
Spring! Who will come to drink this song of purple
wisteria, one flower after another?

The Tranquility Of The Old Alley

How many years has that alley been filled with flowers?
A world hidden in a pot of cooking millet
Under the shade, a child does not sweep the flowers
His innocent smile teases the wanderer with ease
The breeze does not hesitate to come, all around
No low houses, no red bricks
Now, the traveler is lonely, brushing his clothes quietly
He cannot find a single traveler anywhere

Tourists come in and laugh
Each of them is intoxicated in the butterfly flowers
At the foot of the wall, a ground of broken foundations and
plates
Five red brick houses count the countless years
The harbor is not that difficult to understand
The laughter from the walls is mesmerizing
When will the mud be deep enough to live in?
What remains of the old houses is still the same
Where is the vermilion door to come and play again?

The feet stagger, dodging the potholes of dreams that have
returned for fifty years
Since the old alley has already been sold to prosperity
Why rush to come and go?

Shareef Abdur Rasheed

Shareef Abdur-Rasheed, AKA Zakir Flo was born and raised in Brooklyn, New York. His education includes Brooklyn College, Suffolk County Community College and Makkah, Saudi Arabia. He is a Veteran of the Viet Nam era, where in 1969 he reverted to his now reverently embraced Islamic Faith. He is very active in the Islamic community and beyond with his teachings, activism and his humanity.

Shareef's spiritual expression comes through the persona of "Zakir Flo" . Zakir is Arabic for "To remind". Never silent, Shareef Abdur-Rasheed is always dropping science, love, consciousness and signs of the time in rhyme.

Shareef is the Patriarch of the Abdur-Rasheed Family with 9 Children (6 Sons and 3 Daughters) and 41 Grandchildren (24 Boys and 17 Girls).

For more information about Shareef, visit his personal FaceBook Page at :

https://www.facebook.com/shareef.abdurrasheed1
https://zakirflo.wordpress.com

sisters in the bag

Bali near Indonesia
Melati, Isabel
Wijsen sisters
2013 Melati 12
Isabel 10 inspired
class in school
world leaders
activists who took
up vital causes
aware big problem
environmental threat
plastic bags all over
Bali
sisters to the rescue
started petition
clean up plastic bags
Only 5% being recycled
choking Bali's
environment
generated 100,000
signatures
movement on the move
initiative named
Bye Bye Plastic Bags
notoriety grew
generated by a hunger
strike
got attention of Bali's
governor who made
a promise to rid Bali
of plastic by 2018
news of what became

a movement lead by youth
spread worldwide
Chapters of
Bye bye plastic bags
Popped up through out
The region
sisters invited to United
Nations New York 2017
on United Nations World
Ocean Day to speak
Never underestimate
the.
ability of youth

Testimony

on that day when mothers will abandon suckling child,
terrified
sun comes near, mankind immersed in their own sweat
limbs will speak bearing witness to their utilization
tongue gives testimony before the very one that already
knows the answers but still it will give accounts
about what and to whom it near, mankind
others remembered it's maker, thee architect, designer
this day revealed recorded deeds rehearsed letter by letter,
verse by verse, perhaps wonderful, perhaps damning
giving reasons to descend into abyss of fire
genitals confess illicit tryst, consumed by desire
hands will recount how they were directed to reach out
to help, helpless, maybe heal by grace of thee healer
or hurt them with blunt force, torture, traumatize, maim,
murder
violent violations of law, theft ,touching, grabbing, groping
what wasn't theirs or trembling, begging, held high,
supplicating for forgiveness, seeking redemption from
succumbing to temptation, avoiding damnation
ears will tell of what they listened to, maybe gossip,
backbiting,
falsehoods, conversely that which is good, like knowledge
of right and wrong, words of guidance, inspiration to
adhere to,
remind deaf, dumb, blind nations to enjoin
peaceful, loving participation in that which enhance quality
of life
eyes looking at that which steal sight especially insight
essentially blind though physically functionable, spiritually
void due to how they're being employed
they as well will tell and tell..,

as will feet bear witness as to where they went and why
and the owners of these limbs couldn't stop if they tried
believe this or call it a lie but think a moment, really try
do you think there's no rhyme or reason to why we live
and die, meaning void of purpose that's why?
so, what's all the fuss about obeying universal laws that
govern us when right or wrong we all end up with no
punishment or rewards for any of us?
so, throw right and wrong out the window and let's do
whatever we want to?
food for thought to remind you right and wrong is
proven true as is the creator, architect, author that gave
it to you
and dem body parts too
he who created me and you can and will do whatever
he wants to when and how he wants to
just by proclaiming "Be ".........Seeee?

blessed..,

are them who affirms it's true
followed by gratitude
manifest in attitude
quest for truth ensues
test of sincere conviction
least to live contradiction
manifest in *dawah
speaking truth to power
trying to follow through
before your times up
descends on you
puts end to what you can do
putting righteous deeds
in heavenly bank
overseen in unseen
by he who created you
seen and unseen too
heaps rewards on you
ooh how blessed are you
you overcame in the name
of he who created you
protected you, guided you
so that to abided by what's
true
confided only in the one(1)
who made you
knowing that's the only source
to bless you.
him who forgave his slave
though dem failed test
creator gave

*dawah = invite to do right

36

Kimberly Burnham

Kimberly Burnham

A brain health expert with a PhD in Integrative Medicine, Kimberly Burnham has lived in tropical Colombia; in Belgium during the Vietnam War; in Japan teaching businessmen English; in diverse international Toronto, Canada; and several places in the US. Now, she's in Spokane, WA with her wife, Elizabeth, two sets of twins (age 11 & 14) and three dogs. Her recent book, *Awakenings: Peace Dictionary, Language and the Mind, a Daily Brain Health Program* includes the word for peace in hundreds of languages. Her poetry weaves through 80+ volumes of *The Year of the Poet, Inspired by Gandhi, Women Building the World*, and *A Woman's Place in the Dictionary*. She is currently working on several ekphrastic writing projects. One is a novel, *Art Thief Cracks Healing Code for Parkinson's Disease* and the other is non-fiction, *Using Ekphrastic Fiction Writing and Poetry to Create Interest and Promote Artists, Writers, and Poets.*

http://www.NerveWhisperer.Solutions

https://healthy-brain.medium.com/bears-at-the-window-of-climate-change-d1fb403eeaf3

The One Thing

Find the one thing
says Melati Wijsen and her sister Isabel
from which passion flows
find the tangible way
make a difference
so big
even a 10- and 12-year-old can do it
maybe it is bye bye plastic
maybe it is peace
or perhaps clean water
wherever you are
find the one thing
from which passion flows

Love, Joy, Peace

In Balinese, spoken in Bali
"Dame" is peace and the name of a traditional sarong.
wrap yourself in "Dame" or "Kasukan"
or "Awiawahara" always do good with peace and sincerity

"Kapitresnan" is love
and "Kasihin" as well love, care,
invite to be good again
while "Begèr" is passionate love

"Kaliangan" is joy
"Kendel" be happy, be joyful
satisfaction, joy, happiness, gladness
flow from one to the other
from me to you and beyond

The One's Responsibility

There is a word in Javanese
"Têntrême" means peace, peaceful, and safe
in this language of New Caledonia, Java and Bali

"Kê-" means to entrusted (with), assigned (to)
as in "Kang kê- nata têntrême"
the one whose responsibility it is to maintain the peace

Who is the one
we are each the one
responsible for peace

Elizabeth E. Castillo

Elizabeth Esguerra Castillo

Elizabeth Esguerra Castillo is a multi-awarded and an Internationally-Published Contemporary Author/Poet and a Professional Writer / Creative Writer / Feature Writer / Journalist / Travel Writer from the Philippines. She has 2 published books, "Seasons of Emotions" (UK) and "Inner Reflections of the Muse", (USA). Elizabeth is also a co-author to more than 60 international anthologies in the USA, Canada, UK, Romania, India. She is a Contributing Editor of Inner Child Magazine, USA and an Advisory Board Member of Reflection Magazine, an international literary magazine. She is a member of the American Authors Association (AAA) and PEN International.

Web links:

Facebook Fan Page

https://free.facebook.com/ElizabethEsguerraCastillo

Google Plus

https://plus.google.com/u/0/+ElizabethCastillo

Youth Empowerment

Melati and Isabel stunned the world

At an early age, they set good examples to the young

Their contributions cannot be denied

Advocates of environmental awareness,

They banned the use of plastic bags in Bali

Youth empowerment at its finest

These girls are beautiful souls

Making the Earth a better place for generations to come!

A Greener Earth

Lush greeneries abound
Sweet smelling scent of blooming flowers in Spring time
As children play around a beauteous prairie,
The Earth used to be a cooler place to live in
Fresh air we breathe, not much pollution,
When we walk outside to enjoy a Summer's day.
Can we still achieve a greener Earth?
Despite all these toxic things around us,
Man was designated by God to look over His creations
But because of greed for power and money,
He forgot what's his real mission on this planet
Can we ever reverse the amount of pollution?
A greener Earth is what we all dream of
A breath of fresh air when the dawn sets in,
To be surrounded by tall trees with branches
Spreading towards the Heavens as if praying,
For rains to come and shower this arid land
A greener Earth is still possible if we simply take the
initiative!

A New Genesis

In Genesis they held hands together,
A Paradise in unity, love abounds
The Tree of Life stood in their midst
Prohibited by God to get near to it.
Cast away, they walked to the ends of the Earth,
Reincarnated lives continue to haunt their souls
The Tower of Babel they built to reach the Heavens
But God forbade them and off they fell down.
The Great Flood came, vanishing lives in an instant,
A New World emerged, a new age daring flight
The New Adam and Eve built an empire,
Worked hard to achieve whatever they desired.
The haunting of the past continues its saga,
Plagues kept testing the spirit of humankind
The parted Red Sea of blood was a catalyst,
In sending people to a new Promised Land.
But still man was discontented,
Money and riches were all on his mind
Greed over power to him was an adventure,
Until came the Day of Rapture.
Pandemics can alter the lives of many
But not all can experience the Epiphany,
What if all these only test our faith?
And that the dawning of a new Genesis is at hand?
Tomorrow we can witness a brand-new beginning,
Full of hope that we can all survive
That the weary will have confidence in himself,
And the sick will be healed in time.

Joe
Paire

Joe Paire

Joseph L Paire' aka Joe DaVerbal Minddancer . . .
is a quiet man, born in a time where civil liberties
were a walk on thin ice. He's been a victim of his
own shyness often sidelined in his own quest for
love. He became the observer, charting life's path.
Taking note of the why, people do what they do. His
writings oft times strike a cord with the
dormant strings of the reader. His pen the rosined
bow drawn across the mind. He comes full-frontal
or in the subtlest way, always expressing in a way
that stimulate the senses.

www.facebook.com/joe.minddancer

E-Plastic Bags

Falling from a shelf not meant for them.
Parachuting gravity,
what are these billowy things
cavity's filled to the brim,
We don't need more of them.
Beaches by the score implore
Find a solution! End this polution

Defined by children,
knowing how it should've been
Ten and twelve respectively,
Inspired by others respectfully

Except the world is slow to react to facts
Accepting what's easier, like not spending tax
Melati and Isabel Wijsen spoke how they felt
I too, feel certain things are lax.

"To all the kids of this
beautiful but challenging world,
go for it, make that difference"

it's with pride that I make that inference
another closing of the year,
another mother's frozen tears
another reason to give thanks
another season I hope won't be the same
another vote and still I hope,
it's not based on blame
another beach still needs cleaning.

One By One

Removing the shape of game pieces
It takes a steady hand, and a bit of engineering
Who will topple the structure built so carefully
Who will claim winner, as we begin again

I normally cry out cheater,
When one capitalizes on my failure
That makes it fun for me,
but I never shook the table,
I don't play with those people
Don't we all have different labels

Board games for the bored
Does this present a challenge
Bent knees on the floor
Some bet their rent, yet can't handle it
Splinter free wood, smoothed to perfection
Unleveled table, makes it lean toward me
I'm about to cry foul, as a fowl flies by
Judging by its wingspan, it damn sure ain't no owl

I called my friend a buzzard,
He called me what I won't repeat here
It's not my turn, is it?
Was it, isn't improper English
As the jingle of bells grow near
There'll be these pieces all boxed so neat
They'll be happy faces, and a look of, what is this.
One by one, the look of converted minds
I too, was sold on this simple idea.

Battle With Nature

I can't keep up with the fall
The fall of leaves the fall of my serenity
Wind-blown rainstorm from trees

It's a beautiful scene with beautiful scenery
I could supply a million scrapbooks
Oddly shaped leaves spiral down gently

Spinning in circles like a miniature helicopter
Seeds by design fall the same
The leaves in my tines hear my whining complaint

Complacency in statements, as nature waits some
I'm a lazy raker, my efforts, I won't waste none
Waste them?
Bag them and place them on the corner

I won't mourn the loss of what shall bloom again
I'm content with seeing through bare branches
The moon again, I will swoon again for spring
For spring is loves rising, yet still involves leaves

A leaf, a branch, and a tree, we'll spar again
When it's dark earlier than it's been
Mechanically blown, thrown into a firepit
I'll sit in circumference,
feeling the warmth from this pyre
inspired by leaves.

hülya
n.
yılmaz

hülya n. yılmaz

Of Turkish descent, hülya n. yılmaz [sic] is Professor
Emerita (Penn State, U.S.A.), Director of Editing Services
(Inner Child Press International, U.S.A.), and a trilingual
literary translator. Before her poetry and prose publications,
she authored an extensive research book in German on cross-
cultural literary influences.

Her works of literature include a trilingual collection of
poems, memoirs in verse, prose poetry, short stories, a
bilingual poetry book, and two books of poetry (one, co-
authored). Her poetic offerings appeared in numerous
anthologies of global endeavors.

hülya writes creatively to attain and nourish a
comprehensive awareness for and development of our
humanity.

hülya n. yılmaz, a traveler on the journey called "life" . . .

Writing Web Site
https://hulyanyilmaz.com/

Editing Web Site
https://hulyasfreelancing.com

Rwanda and Bali

Whether we call it a Domino-Effect,
or assign a different name to the humanistic impact
that materializes across the globe
in complete disregard of boundaries,
cross-cultural influences do exist.

Rwanda on one hand,
Bali, on the other . . .
5877 miles of a flight-distance—
not exactly neighboring each other!

The first imposes a ban on its citizens in 2008:
No more polyethylene bags!

Thanks to Melati and Isabel Wijsen,
their native island Bali follows suit in 2020:
A legislation, *Restrictions on the Generation of
Disposable Plastic Waste Collection*,
renders it illegal to manufacture, distribute, sell, provide,
and consume
disposable plastics; i.e., plastic bags, Styrofoam, and plastic
straws.

The end-result?
Through a narrow lens . . .
The Republic of Indonesia's Bali province
is officially plastic bag free;

The end-result?
Under a larger observation glass . . .
A growing number of advocates
For reduced plastic use in 15 different countries;

The end-result?
In pursuit of a broader inclusion . . .
The tripling of the number of public policies
to phase out plastic bags between 2010 and 2019,
and the introduction of bans on plastic bags
in 99 countries.

"Bye-Bye Plastic Bags!"

Thus chanted a 10-year-old and
a 12-year-old on the island of Bali.

Their first online petitions resulted in
over 6,000 signatures within a day alone.

Then waved everyone across the Republic of Indonesia
goodbye to the pollution by that environmental foe.

99 countries soon followed in the Indonesian footsteps.

What about the U.S.A.?

Alas!
There is no national plastic bag fee or ban
currently in effect in the United States.

on this joint journey . . .

be a child, my child

be what you are meant to be

always smile broadly

Teresa E. Gallion

Teresa E. Gallion was born in Shreveport, Louisiana and moved to Illinois at the age of 15. She completed her undergraduate training at the University of Illinois Chicago and received her master's degree in Psychology from Bowling Green State University in Ohio. She retired from New Mexico state government in 2012.

She moved to New Mexico in 1987. While writing sporadically for many years, in 1998 she started reading her work in the local Albuquerque poetry community. She has been a featured reader at local coffee houses, bookstores, art galleries, museums, libraries, Outpost Performance Space, the Route 66 Festival in 2001 and the State of Oklahoma's Poetry Festival in Cheyenne, Oklahoma in 2004. She occasionally hosts an open mic.

Teresa's work is published in numerous Journals and anthologies. She has two CDs: *On the Wings of the Wind* and *Poems from Chasing Light*. She has published three books: *Walking Sacred Ground, Contemplation in the High Desert* and *Chasing Light.*

Chasing Light was a finalist in the 2013 New Mexico/Arizona Book Awards.

The surreal high desert landscape and her personal spiritual journey influence the writing of this Albuquerque poet. When she is not writing, she is committed to hiking the enchanted landscapes of New Mexico. You may preview her work at

http://bit.ly/1aIVPNq or *http://bit.ly/13IMLGh*

Mantra for Melati and Isabel

We may sing a mantra for Melati and Isabel.
A sign of respect for the determination of youth
to propel the countries of Bali and Indonesia
into a rally for conscious conservation.

Together they started a wave of activism
to cleanup beaches and advocate
for the reduction in plastic usage.

They won the battle and eliminated plastic bags.
Their future advocacy will no doubt
impact the war on a clean environment.
For this, we sing their names with praise.

For the Fur Babies

The fur babies gather at the river
bow to honor all their furry
brothers and sisters
crossing the rainbow bridge

They each raise a paw to salute them
for completing the journey of love
to support humans unconditionally
in the quest for love.

Now they get to rest and renew
before choosing their next human.
Each paw beats the chest
in gratitude of service.

Ancient Sightings

A songbird serenades my senses
in the Temple of Philae.
I want to fill the hollow space
in my heart with the embrace of Isis.

How can I be here and there
between my high desert home
and the desert of Egypt?
Shape shifting like a hungry ghost,
I can trace hieroglyphics and petroglyphs
running back and forth
between divergent planes.

My breath releases a soul
riding on the fingertips of clouds
above the Valley of the Kings
and the Petroglyph National Monument.

The thunder of color rides
the ship of the desert and
I smile back at those fellows
strutting in the sand.
High top boots strut near my home.

Night approaches like a lost lover
and I am wired from Turkish coffee
screaming through my naked veins.
I must silence the thunder.

American cicadas and ancient
Egyptian scarabs sing loud
in the summer heat of the valleys.
I want to trap this experience
like a clawing honeysuckle
and savor the exposure.

Ashok
K.
Bhargava

ASHOK BHARGAVA is a poet, writer, inspirational speaker and a literary consultant. He has attended poetry conferences in Italy, Turkey, India and Philippines. His latest book "Riding the Tide" about his battle with cancer has been translated and published in Arabic, Hindi, Telugu and Bengali languages. He is a contributing writer to several anthologies worldwide including World Poetry Almanac 2014. He has been published in numerous print and online magazines.

Ashok has won many accolades including Poet Ambassador to Japan, Kalidasa International award, World Poetry Lifetime Achievement award, Writers Beyond Borders Peace award and Tapsilog Leadership award for his community involvement. He is founder of Writers International Network Canada Society to discover, nourish, recognize and celebrate writers, poets and artists and to assist them to network with the community at large. He is the author of eight books of poetry and one anthology. He is Artist-in-Residence at Moberly Arts & Cultural Centre and also co-edits the literary section of The Link Newspaper.

Lack of Moderation

I love
multi-layered cities,
its meandering streets,
nightlights,
poetry readings,
murals,
smartphone whispers.

I hate
its intolerance,
divisions,
car fumes,
traffic jams,
pollution.

In a park
where I sit
trees stand high
a river of plastic bags
flows by me
in silence.

Desire

She was sad
tear stained face
and silent.

Without turning
she lifted her chin up
and asked
had I seen an ant
dragging away the wings of a butterfly?

No, I answered.

That's good, could I write or compose?
What? I asked.
A poem: a poem enticing a lover to make love
Why? I inquired.
I will shred it into a million pieces and burn it
She said.
Then without uttering a word,
she got up
and left
leaving behind silence.

Terracotta Passion

I live
like a Banyan root
hanging
waiting
to reach the earth
for soil to cling to
for nourishment
for rootedness.

Without you
I am
hovering
waiting for your hands
to hold me
to infuse hope
to energize
to begin life.

With you
I feel alive
I embrace you
like a Banyan root
that has reached the earth
and connected
to the soil.

Caroline
'Ceri Naz'
Nazareno
Gabis

Caroline 'Ceri' Nazareno-Gabis

Caroline 'Ceri Naz' Nazareno-Gabis, author of Velvet Passions of Calibrated Quarks, World Poetry Canada International Director to Philippines is a multi-awarded poet, editor, journalist, educator, peace and women's advocate. She believes that learning other's language and culture is a doorway to wisdom.

Among her poetic belts include **Gabrielle Galloni Memorial Panorama International Youth Award 2022**, Panorama Youth Literary Awards 2020, 7th Prize Winner in the 19th, 20th and 21st Italian Award of Literary Festival; Writers International Network-Canada ''Amazing Poet 2015'', The Frang Bardhi Literary Prize 2014 (Albania), Poet Journalist Award 2014 (Tuzla, Istanbul, Turkey) and World Poetry Empowered Poet 2013 (Vancouver, Canada). She's a featured member of Association of Women's Rights and Development (AWID), The Poetry Posse, Galaktika Poetike, Asia Pacific Writers and Translators (APWT), Axlepino and Anacbanua. Her poetry and children's stories have been featured in different anthologies and magazines worldwide.

Links to her works:

http://panitikan.ph/2018/03/30/caroline-nazareno-gabis/

https://apwriters.org/author/ceri_naz/

http://www.aveviajera.org/nacionesunidasdelasletras/id1181.html

Ocean Deep

Two Bali babies who fell deeply in love
With the gift of flowing pristine water,
And all the wonders that it holds,
It mirrors their deepest mission
To have plastic-free ocean,
Believing that all creatures
Under the sea are all precious,
Interconnected waves,
The calming salty breeze,
Magical habitat—
It's worth fighting for.
Young but high-spirited bellas
Racing to save the incredible treasure
The ocean of life and for life,

I am becoming more and more

I am becoming more believing and more reliving
With the kindness shared, the hearts you filled
With goodness,
I am more relieved,
Because I know you're there.

I am becoming more understanding and more
knowledgeable
Because you share your wisdom
You lift me up from the uncertainties,
That you become the compass
Of my wandering thoughts.

I am becoming more grateful and more gracious
Because of the unwavering support
And unconditional love,
You make the impossible possible
Within my reach,
Because you make me believe,
I can do all things,
With you, the powerhouse of my energy.

My Sweet Little Boss

I came from school
With a heavy headache,
Almost drowsy and feeling clumpsy,
I sat down, closed my eyes,
My sweet little boss said,
''I want to hold you, mom,
So you will feel better''

I told her, Thank you, my sweet girl,
You're acting as if you are a true doctor,
She held my hand, giving her milk bottle,
I smiled, asked for water instead
She gave me the warmest embrace,
I love my sweet little boss,
My daughter's purest love.

Swapna Behera

Swapna Behera is a trilingual poet, translator, environmentalist, editor from India and author of seven books of different genres including one on children's literature on Environment. She is the recipient of International UGADI AWARD 2019, honoured from Gujarat Sahitya Akademi 2022, 2021 International Poesis Award of Honor as Jury, Pentasi B World Fellow Poet, Honoured Poet of India from Seychelles Government and International awards from Algeria, Morocco, Kajhakhstan, modern Arabic Literary Renaissance of Egypt, International Arts Council Argentina etc. Her stories, poems, articles are published in many International and National magazines and ezines. Her poem A NIGHT IN THE REFUGEE CAMP is translated into 67 languages. She has received over 60 National and International Awards. At present she is the Cultural Ambassador for India and South Asia of Inner Child and the life member of Odisha Environmental Society

Email
swapna.behera@gmail.com

Web Site
http://swapnabehera.in/

"Bye bye plastic bags" say Melati and Isabel Wijsen

children prodigy they are
Melati and Isabel
decreased the global use of single use plastics
inspired by the Rwanda's ban on polythene
climate activists they are
sisters born in Bali to Dutch and Indonesian parents
someone has to raise the voice
to save and sustain Mother Nature
they tried it in Bali their native place
a message that travelled from Rwanda to Bali
beach clean ups, Government petitions accelerated the
drive
Bali is officially plastic free because of them
Wijsen will lead for Indonesia
some where some one is thinking for a safe environment
they were only twelve and ten
when they started campaign for the world
free of plastic bags through education
political meetings ,campaigns and youth empowerment
don't ever wait for age or permission to start a mission
will tomorrow be made of plastics?
will we be dumped in the graveyard of plastics…?

if you are with me……

when you are with me
the sky bows
death flows reverse
river becomes pregnant
sparrow's nest swings in palm tree
rice plants carry paddy
consciousness stands boldly
no abscission of spring
words become crazy
all orders are transmitted
if you are with me
fire is frozen
sandalwood spreads fragrances
birds twit; fears evaporate
illusions get salvation
solitude appeals for liberty
and creates new languages
the ugliest becomes the diva
clay gets life
if you are with me
I forget and my memory is deleted
the formulae of all mathematics is lost
my ego is immersed
explosion occurs
I swing between your lost and found
because at the end of this journey I am ordained
with dignity I become you
I become yours truly
I become The Goddess

my mother's pandora box

you find safety pins ,candies, fur or seeds
white hairs stuck to that
she touches it every day
and feels the existence of my father
she is ninety four ;the walking encyclopaedia
cooking or food preservation
jam, jelly ,seasons or values
she knows how to imbibe or sustain
a former badminton captain ,excellent speaker
now lean and thin , skin above the Skelton
still has the interest and opinion for games ,politics
she is the youngest Diva for me
my mother has become my daughter
time changes the relationship
struggling though with ageing process
an empowered lady with ethics, values
a good orator's voice is feeble
but contents are robust
we both talk about death and life
hold our hands and smile together
who cares death by the way …!!!

Albert 'Infinite' Carrasco

Albert "Infinite The Poet" Carrasco is an urban poet, mentor and public speaker.

Albert believes his experience of growing up in poverty, dealing with drugs and witnessing murder over and over were lessons learnt, in order to gain knowledge to teach. Albert's harsh reality and honesty is a powerfully packed punch delivered through rhyme. Infinite grew up in the east part of the Bronx and still resides there, so he knows many young men will follow the same dark path he followed looking for change. The life of crime should never be an option to being poor but it is, very often.

Infinite poetry @lulu.com

Alcarrasco2 on YouTube

Infinite the poet on reverbnation

Infinite Poetry

www.lulu.com/us/en/shop/al-infinite-carrasco/infinite-poetry/paperback/product-21040240.html

www.innerchildpress.com/albert-carrasco

Melati and Isabel Wijsen

What were we supposed to do? sit back and watch a problem get bigger right in front of our eyes? watch it rise? No, my sister and I wanted to take part in the solution of ending Indonesia's plastic pollution. When we found out that only 5% of the plastic bags in Bali were being recycled, we wanted to change that, it was time for a clean up revolution. Of course it couldn't be done with just my sister and i, we needed the help of leaders and the community to spread awareness of a global nuisance. At just 10 and 12 years old we began a clean up campaign and we weren't going to stop until we reached our goal. We petitioned for signatures and had presentations to gather up needed attention on how important it is to stop the sales of plastic bags in turn for alternatives. "Bye Bye plastic bags" is something my sister and i started and became a social initiative, that was our part of making Bali and places all over the world affected by this problem a better place to live. With the help of the media our voices were heard in different areas. our movement gained momentum with the help of TED, CNN and the united nations. In 2013 we became familiar with the plastic pollution problem, in 2018 our hard work alongside others working together to make our world better helped make the ban of single use plastic bags out of our daily curriculum.

Harsh

Living through so much harsh treatment , so many harsh conditions, cause me to see nothing but bright visions. My interpretation of life was like that of one that lived in hell, when I narrate I speak of how hell fucked me so others can be celibate, before jurors and magistrates, before a barrage of bullets, skipping triage straight to emergency for blood currency. I live with pain and hatred not toward people but at all the things I did and things that was done and can't be unwoven, I go to cemeteries now as a 40 year old man looking at the first to die, they were children. Born in the 70's died in the 80's we were crack babies but moms weren't smoking, we were young coke cookers, pack pushers, Gat toters, we held down blocks till eternal resting spots, that's why i stare at kids faces carved on marble rock. I visit plots with moms and pops with the last sibling the same age as the one no longer living. I know it's hard for consumption, it consumed me, it moved me to push my pen on paper and relive my past, ghetto music, wood wind and brass of the aftermath of living fast.

Eyes

Have you ever been looked at from dead eyes? I have. I've been looked at by many with those eyes. Its look is just as yesterday, same expression. It's an I'll state of mind knowing any second any minute maybe within the hour, might be their time. Imagine the one starring at you doesn't know they're going to die. but... you..you soon find out that you were looking at dead eyes.. How would that feel? Let me explain. It's surreal. I gave him a hug and a kiss, daddy I love you don't ever leave me, he looked at me while holding me, na "ace" I'm not going no place... Don't worry daddy I remember that look and your voice. I knew you would of still been here if you had a choice. It's midnight.. Al look I bought this gun! I didn't take it because like him I had a fascination with them.. He stared at me holding that gun... It's three in the morning now I mourn him. Dude I got love for you but these guys around here don't know you. Al I grew up here just like you. Yeah I understand but you moved. we kept contact these cats don't remember you. They're hungry. you eating off their plate is not safe, to them your a stranger, go back to Miami with your mother! He looked at me with those eyes, na al I'm gonna stay and make a killing.. He did.. He made a killer kill him. R.I.P. to him. Why did they have to look at me with those eyes?...

Michelle

Joan

Barulich

Michelle Joan Barulich

Michelle Joan Barulich was born in Honolulu, Hawaii on the island of Oahu. She started writing poetry and songs with her younger brother Paul. They have written many songs in their teen years. She is currently studying Alternative Medicine and would like to become a Homeopathic Doctor. Michelle loves all kinds of animals and birds; she does wild rehabilitation. She has also rescued rock pigeons that make great pets.

https://www.facebook.com/michelle.barulich

Melati and Isabel

Two sisters working together
Brainstorming ideas to help the climate
To reduce plastic consumption in Bali
Hard work and determination
Signatures on paper
To insight the people
To say bye bye plastic bags
Driven by youth
Your message received
All around the world
Way to go Melati and Isabel!

Unspoken Words

Sad songs that I listen to
Funny how I think of you
Before you left there was so many words
You wanted to say
But no one would listen
There was so many feelings
You wanted to touch
But no one could care that much
I hear my crying out loud
Each tear means something to me
And if the light of the dawn breaks first
Will you still leave?
with unspoken words unleft to say
I can hear voices in your head
There calling your name
I can come in touch with your fears
I can retrace yesterday's heartaches
For I understand
There was so many unspoken words
To be revealed, now they lye in the dead....

Love is the Word

See no diamonds in the sky
We all wanted to understand why
Pick up the pieces and began again
Realizing the mistakes, we have made
Why must we try then lose the nerve?
Searching for the way into my heart
But ignoring the word that makes the start
Love is the word that should be heard
From coast to coast and around the world
All around the world
The people's faces are so sad
All around the world
The countries are so mad
That's why this song is going to make you scream and
shout
Love is the word that should be heard
From coast to coast and around the world
I hope they hear our message
They soon will take
No more nothing if they push the button
No more time to reconsider
Love is the word that should be heard
From coast to coast and around the world
Everybody, love is the word that should be heard
From coast to coast and around the world.

Eliza Segiet

Eliza Segiet graduated with a Master's Degree in Philosophy at Jagiellonian University.

Received *Global Literature Guardian Award* – from Motivational Strips, World Nations Writers Union and Union Hispanomundial De Escritores (UHE) 2018.

Nominated for the Pushcart Prize 2019, 2021.

Laureate *Naji Naaman Literary Prize 2020*,

International Award Paragon of Hope (2020),

World Award 2020 *Cesar Vallejo* for Literary Excellence. Laureate of the Special Jury *Sahitto International Award* 2021, World Award *Premiul Fănuş Neagu* 2021.

Finalist *Golden Aster Book* World Literary Prize 2020, *Mili Dueli* 2022, Voci nel deserto 2022.

At the international Festival of Poetry CAMPIONATO MONDIALE DI POESIA (2021/2022) she won the title of vice-champion of the world.

Award BHARAT RATNA RABINDRANATH TAGORE INTERNATIONAL AWARD (2022).

Award - *World Poets Association* (2023).

Laureate Between words and infinity *"International Literary Award (2023).*

Resuscitation

Between the plastic bags,
grains shine through
– once called –
golden beach.

What is left of it is the sea of plastic!
Rustling with every gust of wind,
breaks the seaside silence,
doesn't let you relax your mind and
rest.

Young people already know
– it's time to act!

Reanimation of golden sands
will let the living, those thoughtful and reflectionless,
breathe a sigh of relief,
and start the plastic abstinence
right away,
following the words of Melati and Isabel Wijsen:

– *Bye Bye Plastic Bags*

Nature
expects to be freed of spaces
filled with ugly
poisonous artifacts.

Translated by Dorota Stępińska

Bald Words

You had many plans –
all for later.

And she thought
that a miracle will happen.
You told her –
your bald words,
words like checks without cover.

She was sure
it would be just like you promised.
She never dared to ask:
when will it be new?
Yet you
did not have any plans.

You knew
that you will not make change in your life!

Translated by Artur Komoter

Dance

Her eyes said that
she wants to dance,
have fun, go crazy.

Perhaps
she envied others –
of their dancing feet.

She envelops in infirmity –
she cried.

Nobody saw her tears,
nobody saw that
like others
she craves for life.

Maybe he did not want to see?

Translated by Artur Komoter

William S. Peters Sr.

Bill's writing career spans a period of over 50 years. Being first Published in 1972, Bill has since went on to Author in excess of 50 additional Volumes of Poetry, Short Stories, etc., expressing his thoughts on matters of the Heart, Spirit, Consciousness and Humanity. His primary focus is that of Love, Peace and Understanding!

Bill says . . .

I have always likened Life to that of a Garden. So, for me, Life is simply about the Seeds we Sow and Nourish. All things we "Think and Do", will "Be" Cause and eventually manifest itself to being an "Effect" within our own personal "Existences" and "Experiences" . . . whether it be Fruit, Flowers, Weeds or Barren Landscapes! Bill highly regards the Fruits of his Labor and wishes that everyone would thus go on to plant "Lovely" Seeds on "Good Ground" in their own Gardens of Life!

to connect with Bill, he is all things Inner Child

www.iaminnerchild.com

Personal Web Site

www.iamjustbill.com

The Plastic Death

Around the world
Upon land and in oceans
We see fit to
Discard our plastics
Only to further the death
Of a world
We once knew

Grocery stores and other too
See it as a convenience

We once had paper bags,
But they are too costly

Trees felled
Lands cleared
Because we need paper

There is hemp they say,
But if we grow it
Will we use it
As a bio-degradable
Self-sustaining alternative
Or just smoke it
Instead

When all the whales, dolphins and turtles are dead.
Perhaps we will remember
The efforts and
The words said
By Melati and Isabel Wijsen
About "The Plastic Death"

Longing

I long for the time
When caring is not a burden;
Where empathy and compassion
Is effortless;
When love is like the ether
It is everywhere

I wish to live in a world
Where the smiles of the children
Do not depart
Even unto and beyond
Old age and death

I long for the time
When the only wars we struggle through
Is the war of giving,
The war of humanity enacted
And we fight only
To embrace

I long for the time
When the angst of our differences
Becomes a distant memory
And all we see are
Similarities and likeness

I know to some,
This is but a fantasy,
But was not
The Wizard of Oz
Real?

Yes, I believe in M & M's,
The sweetness of
Magic and Miracles,

And we all could do
For a few
Right now ...
Don't you think?

I long for parity
And the cessation of divide
Between
'The Haves and Have-nots'
......
I know this may sound
A bit like a Socialistic preposition,
But what can possibly be wrong
With EVERYONE being OK?

I long for good water
For everybody;
A roof over everyone's head;
Equality in Healthcare and education
And so much more

I long to have the courage
To confront my higher self
And entice id to help me
Overcome my 'self'

I long to challenge and defeat
My lazy procrastination ....
Well, maybe tomorrow

There are so many things
That I long for,
And so many more
That I could,
But what I truly long for
Is to no longer have any
Longing

The Fruits of Trust

I petitioned my Muses
To bring to me
The gift of words
For i wanted to write about
'The Fruits of Trust'

I am a witness
To the wonderful bounty and booty
Yielded unto those
Who are so blessed
To give
And to recieve
This divine state of being

In seeing the fruits
Of the seeds we plant
Of 'Trust'
How can you not exclaim
To the world,
To all creation
Its sweetness

Trust is an ingredient
Widely applied
In relationship...
And encounters....
Those of love,
Those of friendship,
Those of some strangers
And some family members
As well

I tell you,
It is better to have trust
Than not,
After all,
Who wants a life of wariness and weariness ...
'Tis not a good way
To live

Yes, 'Trust'
Is a wonderfully sweet
Ambrosiatic quality
That all should experience
At least once,
In their lives ...
But I say,
Why not vie to have it
Throughout our lives ...

As I said
I can attest that
The Fruits of Trust
Are sweet

December

2023

Featured Poets

~ * ~

Caroline Laurent Turunc

Neha Bhandarkar

Shafkat Aziz Hajam

Elarbi Abdelfattah

i FLY

because I Can

... said the Dreamer to the world.

www.iamjustbill.com

Caroline

Laurent

Turunc

Caroline LAURENT Turunc Antakya, Turkey, Arab origin, the daughter of a family of nine children. She started writing at the age of 15. She wrote her first novel at this age and her family did not allow the book to be published, her brother and mother destroyed the manuscript.

This incident did not prevent her from writing more. She has written over 1500 poems since 2013, received many certificates from abroad, and participated in 12 local and foreign anthologies. Her poems have been published in many international journals and sites. She is writing a novel and is about to finish it soon. She published two poetry books, "Between Oriental and Schemal" and "Desert lily".

She won the second place among 2575 poets from every country during the championship of the world literature in Romania. She won a prize in the poetry festival held by Yan in China which led her to be selected into the "world poet Literature Museum" built by the Silk Road Cultural Center of Northwest University of China. She was also a jury member of the Galaxia International Award for unpublished Poetry, 2021 edition in Chile.

She is a Turkey-based Humanitarian and represents the u.t.e.f. International foundation in Paris. She currently lives in Paris, France

carolineturunc@yahoo.com

Malalai of Maiwand

Malala, you are a true heroine

Proclaimed as Youngest Nobel Prize Laureate

Blossomed from his father's thoughts

 and humanitarian works,

You were loved, Malala.

You woke up those wounded spirits

Who were buried in deep slumber

Of fear, hopelessness and vanished dreams,

Your advocacy on education for girls

And human rights have transformed

The leaders and the youth,

Your light shine in all corners of the globe.

hidden treasure

you left to win and gain
lasting memories,
exhilarating captures
when nature calls,
from sweeping meanders,
from the lush of greens,
from the sulfury smell
of the enthralling coast,
 from the intimate sacred chamber,
that replenishes & sanctifies
wounded souls,
from all walks of life,
been here and there,
sometimes lost,
but never forsaken;
for always
you are the treasure
from the forest of words.

Decoding the Academic Regalia and "Abaray na Dayew"

Behind the cameras, tears poured down,
but it meant a glorious victory over grief, stress,
 anxieties and obstacles.
Behind those filtered smiles,
 I missed my lost loved ones.
I am offering this achievement to them.
The value of encouragement, empowerment,
 and dedication were my powerhouse
 to move forward to finish this journey;
 there was a lag, but I believed, there is always time.
I fervently prayed for guidance,
patience, courage, and determination
 for I trusted the process
because a monumental change
is just right behind the rainbows of willpower;
The John Knox's cap over our heads,
the gowns embracing our bodies,
 with the emblems inspired by the rule of time,
honor, our heritage, and privileges
 remind us how great the change has been,
until we walk the road for a while,
looking back, we see how far we have come
the odyssey to humility and the heart of humanity.

Neha

Bhandarkar

Neha Bhandarkar is trilingual authour and translator. She is columnist in Marathi newspaper. Her 13 books in Marathi, Hindi and English have been published. She is recipient of many most prestigious literary awards from India, like State Hindi Sahitya Academi and bagged awards from foreign countries also. Her many poems and stories are being published in many anthologies, journals, E Zines and magazines in all over the world. Her many poetries, stories have been translated in several foreign languages i.e. French, Albanian, Phillipines, Nepali, Greece, English. As well as Indian languages like Odia, Asamese, Telugu, Bengali, hindi, Brail etc. Her poems and short stories have broadcast on All India Radio, Akashwani, Hindi Radio, Chicago (U.S.A.), Radio France (FRANCE) etc.

Unattached

Giving no heed or precaution
of acceptance and rejection
she simply destines
to string a chain of creation
unceasingly, seamlessly

Protecting and germinating the seed
is the only obligating task to her
laden with such Sanskaras
suffocates her existence

Caressing every passerby
connotes killing her seed
or the carnage of offshoots
even she doesn't know
the sept of misconception of misery
But she knows her own destiny
served on a silver platter
like a plumage shedded peacock

Her sufferings never ward off
nor she can be relieved
even she observes
the 'unattachment'
same as between earth and sky
as a plot of a lot

Her innocent pollens
get churned out
while she procreates intensely
with an unattached mind
and when it becomes indispensable

to give birth to another feminine form
the chain of creation
gets strung automatically

Sheerly in the name of subsistence!....

Setting Down

'O' dearest Poem!
please do commit
to the poets around the world
that never will you die out
coz if you wane, so do the poets

Have you seen the sun fearful
or the moon finished?

O dear!
in the circumstantial dark and glow
countless efforts would be made
to annihilate you
Even so you rise again and again
as the sun and the moon
with a new ray of hope everytime

Like a sweet cuckoo
recognise the onset of spring
Affix the fragments of time
with the cultured civilizations
and enthron the hearts of every one

Be as aromatic as the blue lotus
Be as fragrant as
the essence of musk
Keep waving your stole
with this blossoming land

Shower your pitter-patter
as the writing flow of poets

gush relentlessly drifted away as a river
and keep sailing wantonly
on the word-ferry

I know it is not easy
to keep safe your existence
in the ocean-like Word-web
Even so, you try
Try that you never set-down

It is said,
"The world rests on endurance and hope".

Intolerant

An intolerant moment
intersecting the death and solitude...

From this moment
reaching to the conscience
are innumerable sound-bound
silent thoughts

The setting clouds
peeping through large skylines
uninterruptedly look forward
to taking place
precisely in such untoward moments
in the wasteland
made of solitude and dejection
....Absolutely being all carefree

In the illusioned space of mind
In the caress of solitude
with the dreams of death abound
mingling with melancholy songs
creating a rampage
in the poems
and at such juncture
tolerance evolves
out of a work of art
that intolerant moment
(intersecting death and solitude)
as if; gets killed
....Once again in a city of concrete!

Shafkat

Aziz

Hajam

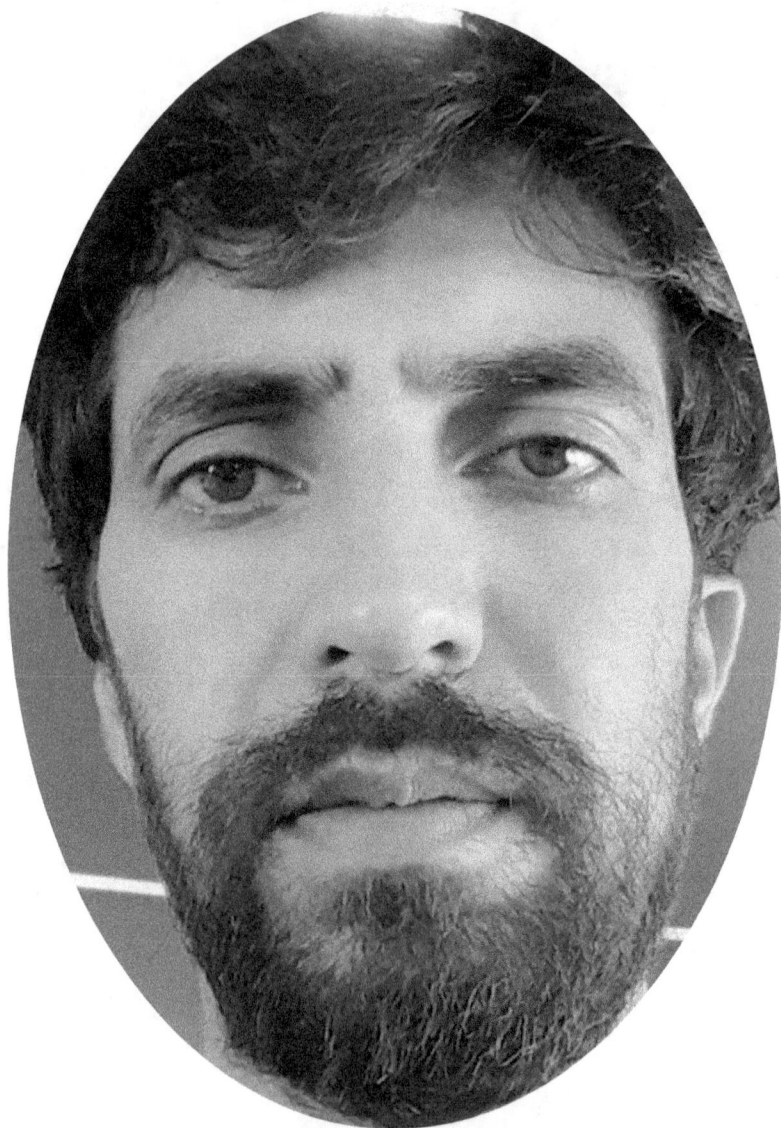

Shafkat Aziz Hajam is a children's Poet from India, kashmir.He is the author of two children poetry books that mostly give a religious touch , titled as The cuckoo's voice and the canary's voice.

Though my skin is black,

Though my skin is black,
My intentions are green.
Let me put them into practice
Colors of joys will be all around seen.
Let me uproot the thorns of hatred,
Let me sow the seeds of love ,
Peace will be enjoyed everywhere
Everyone will symbolize it like a dove .
In the hearts of people, let me
Put out the fire of greed.
All will take their fair share
Of the things they need .
Let me tie people with
The bonds of brotherhood
Let me teach them humanity.
All will be just and will act as they should.

I Am A Book.

I am a book when you read me ,

The whole world you'll see.

You'll visit the snowy mountains

And the deserts where it hardly rains.

You'll visit the bottoms of the deepest Oceans,

You'll enjoy the cultures of different nations.

You'll visit the stars and the moon

And the Earth's hot and cold zone .

You'll visit the palaces of the past kings ,

I will help you to fly around the world

As I am your wings .

This poem is written for my little student,
Yusra ,class Pre Nursery.

O Canary!

Soon thou wilt abandon me ,o canary !

My elated heart wilt become glum, o canary!

Thou wilt visit me in spring,

Till then in my garden who'll sing?

Can not endure thy absence , o canary !

My heart wilt beat but with no rhythm

Thy memories wilt keep me restless,

Until thy arrival there wilt be no charm , o canary !

Elarbi

Abdelfattah

Elarbi Abdelfattah

Curriculum Vitae: Abdel-Fattah Al-Arabi, Tunisian, with a diploma in programmer and analysis in media Doctor of Human Sciences from Université Théophanie International Political and human rights activist, activist and union official, legal advisor at the court Cultural advisor at the Union of Arab Unity Meeting for Poetry and Culture in the Arab World in the Diaspora, Holland Branch Director of the Tunis office of the newspaper Director of the magasine REVISTA AMERICA Sin Fronteras in tunez Responsible for the Équipe de réseautage / activation du Monde Arabe team at the European International Foundation for Peace and Human Rights: Member of the Third Millennium Renaissance - Participated in Poetry Nights in Dhaka (the world's poets in the 100th evening of Odan Little TV magazine countries. - I gave a lecture at the Arab Youth Forum in London, - I gave a lecture and poem at the cultural café in Sulaymaniyah Published in many newspapers I am in the process of preparing to publish my first poetry collection.

Fire in my skull

Sixty years of war burning in my skull
Between thoughts that illuminate the road and others that
extinguish the light
Between tribes from myself and others from outside my life
Skull, put out the blazing fire!
This war foretells destruction
How many books have you read about conflict?
Have you studied poetry theory?
intracranial boiling, screaming, barking
A hustle and bustle, a mixture of the snarling of the seas
Have you made a ruling?
I wrote how many poems on the wall
Is your hair gray or has it escaped your scalp?
Lots of ideas
And I played you with the friction chain
ancient interracial
And a long life history
Without a goal, but coordinated with a torrent of grinding
words
Incomprehensible and rejoicing in murky water
Has time turned to an inevitable end?
Oh time, how treacherous are you?
From the beginning years a skull packed with written
karatis
With talismans, squares, triangles and drawings
How long do we have to fill this skull?
Unconsciously and deciphering secrets
I read all the books of incantations and magic
And the world and the cities swept over
I was not able to know the great knowledge
I do not appreciate the past tense
I am unable to comprehend a future that the Almighty
Creator knows

Meditation

Doors opened from all over the place
on all edges
Foretold all paths
And I alerted all the orbiters
Where are you Sirian?
captured in a valley
I know you exist
in hand
Those mysterious remote commandos
oblivion
Covering between death and another life
Enjoying eternal bliss
in the transfiguration
And a clear look
Unfold on doors that seem open
But it's closed
Opens through a hidden theology
A world that swims and slumps from above
don't realize it
Meditate between unknown times
The mutterings flow from you
And the signs go with you
Perceive sensory places
It has an eternal whisper
unconscious things
You are in the presence of the showers
the darkness of the darkness
Do not know
missing things
I am nothing but a mirage
Swim between the lobbies
Meditate here and there

You are not and there is nothing
Except for existence
who contemplates the loss
the infinite
extending endlessly
It's the loss

chime the bells

Ringing and ringing
coming from above
shake your head up
You see nothing but the echo
Singing into melodies all over your head
You look at yourself and you only see an idol
Nothing has moved for years
stop everything
You hear words here and there
Just talk and action
Nothing is moving
The idol is looking at us
He's moving that idol
But we are in our places
We hear bells ringing everywhere
We walk but we stand where we are
We peek at each other
Sometimes whispering and other advice
We have a void left
full of air
The bells still ring in us
but we are a fetish
We only move in the void
We're writhing in a whirlwind storm
And twist everything in us
Even our minds, our hopes and our dreams
Lose the flavor of life and reap
Green and dry crops
In our roots rip our veins
sucks our blood
Empty inside us and keep us cage
People imprison us

Remembering

our fallen soldiers of verse

Janet Perkins Caldwell

February 14, 1959 ~ September 20, 2016

Alan W. Jankowski

16 March 1961 ~ 10 March 2017

The Butterfly Effect

"IS" in effect

Inner Child Press

News

Published Books

by

Poetry Posse Members

We are so excited to share and announce a few of the current books, as well as the new and upcoming books of some of our Poetry Posse authors.

On the following pages we present to you ...

Alicja Maria Kuberska

Jackie Davis Allen

Gail Weston Shazor

hülya n. yılmaz

Nizar Sartawi

Elizabeth E. Castillo

Faleeha Hassan

Fahredin Shehu

Kimberly Burnham

Caroline 'Ceri' Nazareno

Eliza Segiet

Teresa E. Gallion

William S. Peters, Sr.

Now Available

www.innerchildpress.com

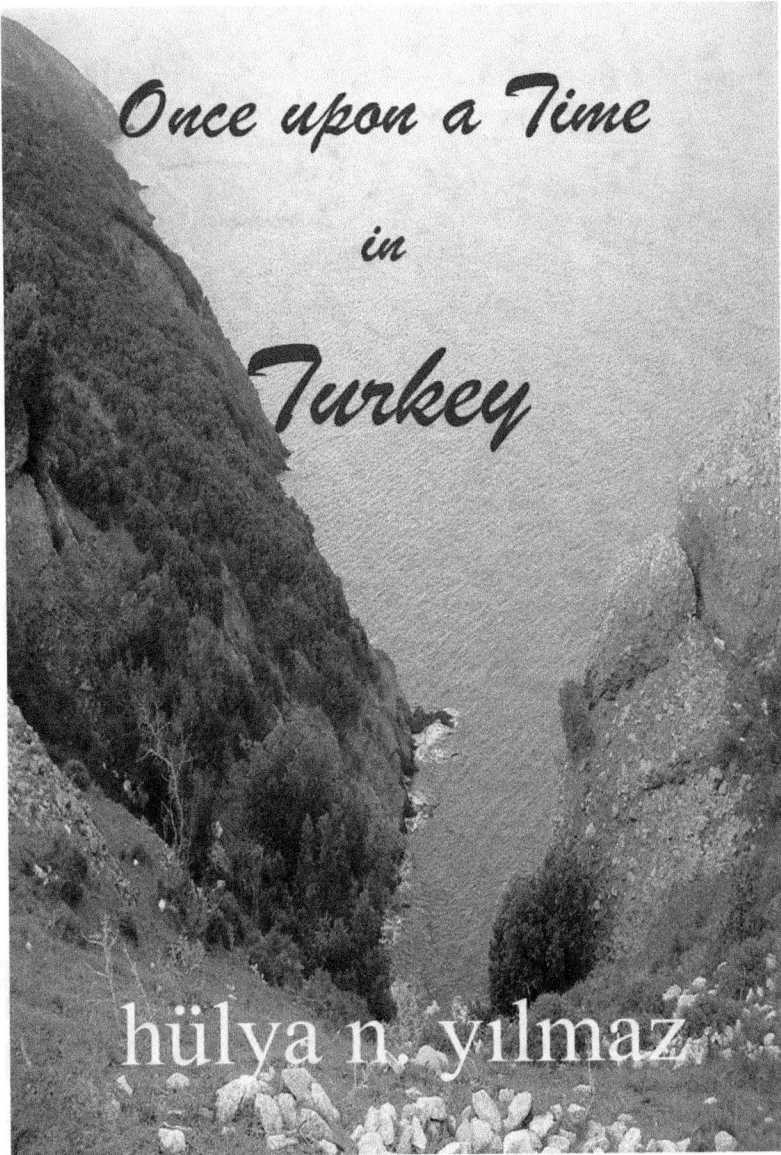

Once upon a Time in Turkey

hülya n. yılmaz

Now Available

www.innerchildpress.com

Unapologetically

BLACK

&

Blues

william s. peters, sr.

Now Available
www.innerchildpress.com

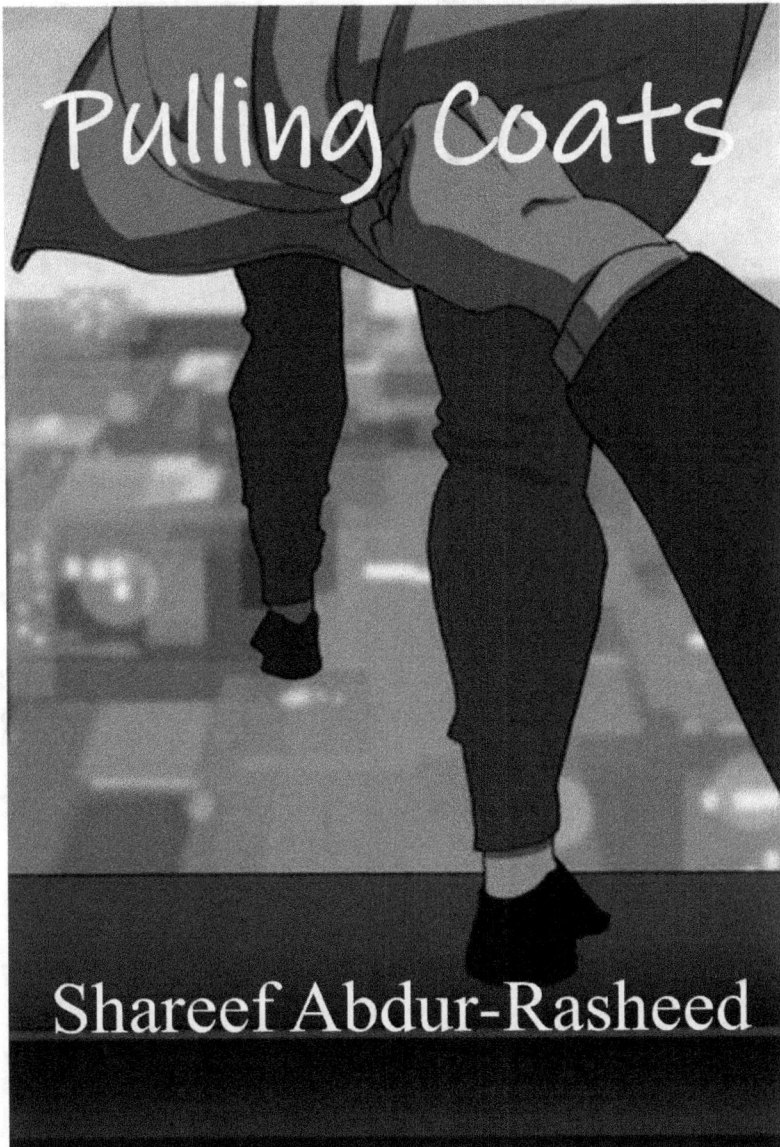

Pulling Coats

Shareef Abdur-Rasheed

Now Available
www.innerchildpress.com

UMAMI
The Essence of Deliciousness

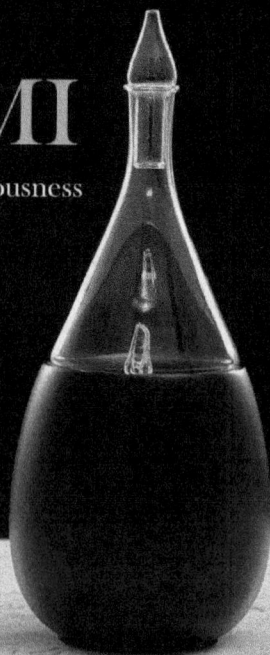

Fahredin Shehu

Now Available

www.innerchildpress.com

After the Frost

Alicja Maria Kuberska

Now Available

www.innerchildpress.com

Fahredin Shehu

ORMUS

Now Available
www.innerchildpress.com

Ahead of My Time

. . . from the Streets to the Stages

Albert 'Infinite' Carrasco

Now Available
www.innerchildpress.com

Eliza Segiet

To Be More

Now Available at

www.amazon.com/gp/product/B08MYL5B7S/ref=
dbs_a_def_rwt_hsch_vapi_tkin_p1_i2

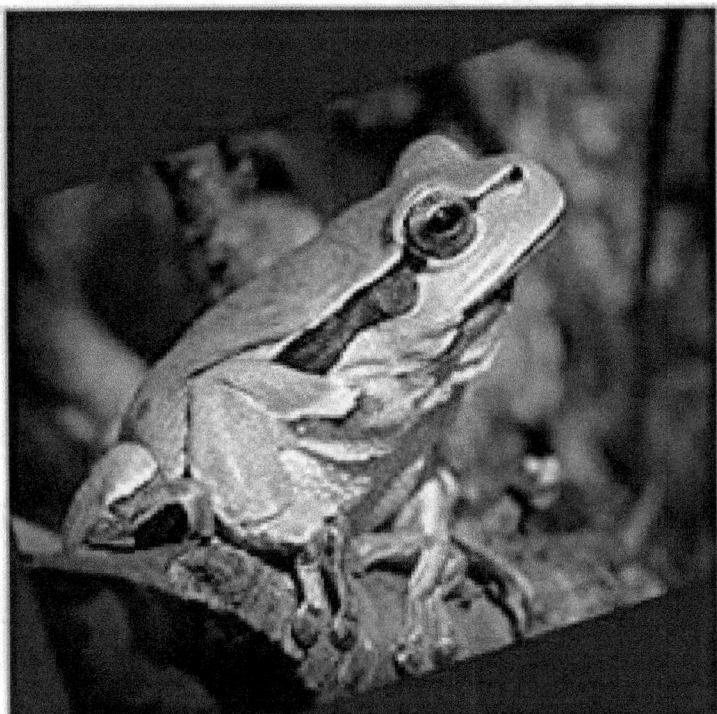

SEARCH FOR THE MAGICAL MULTILINGUAL FROG

A Tale of Ribbit in 50 Languages

KIMBERLY BURNHAM

Now Available at
www.innerchildpress.com

Inner Child Press News

Scent of Love

Poetry by

Teresa E. Gallion

Now Available
www.innerchildpress.com

Inner Reflections
of the
Muse

Elizabeth Castillo

Now Available
www.innerchildpress.com

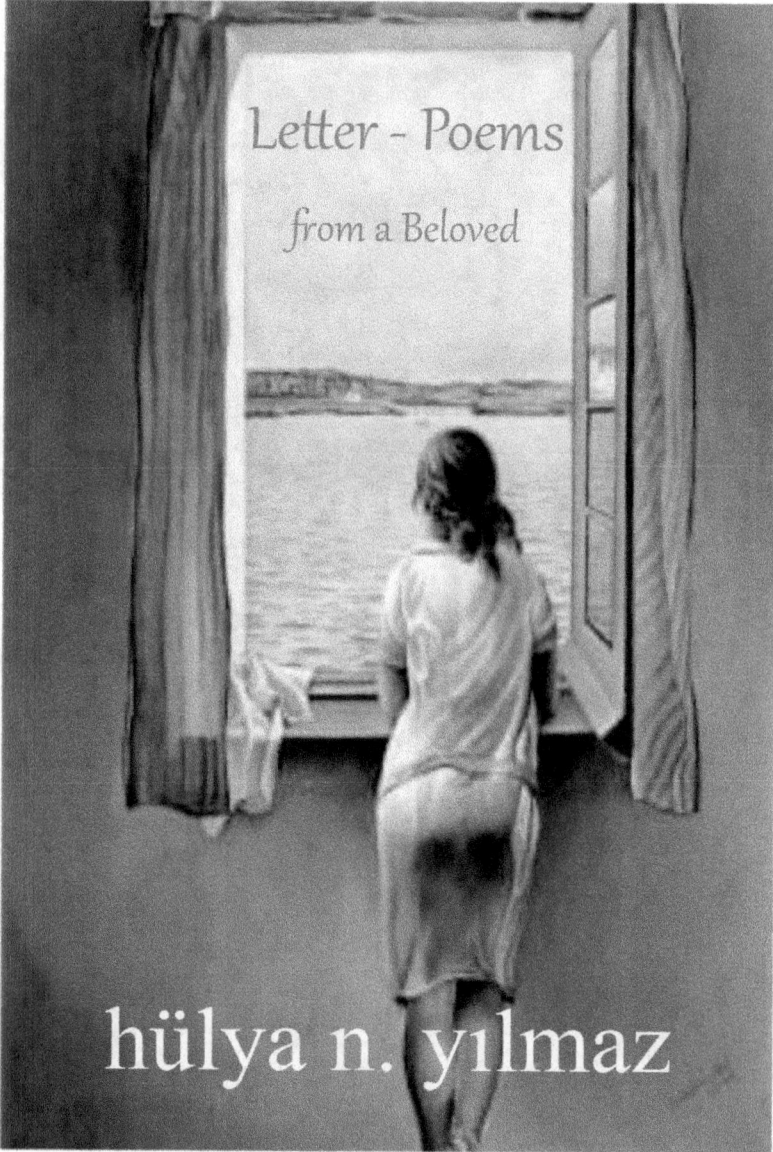

Letter - Poems

from a Beloved

hülya n. yılmaz

Now Available
www.innerchildpress.com

Now Available

www.innerchildpress.com

One Eye Open

u n i r 1.

william s. peters, sr

Now Available
www.innerchildpress.com

The Book of krisar

volume v

william s. peters, sr.

Now Available

www.innerchildpress.com

The Book of krisar

Volume I

william s. peters, sr.

The Book of krisar

Volume II

william s. peters, sr.

Now Available

www.innerchildpress.com

The Book of krisar

Volume III

william s. peters, sr.

The Book of krisar

Volume IV

william s. peters, sr.

Now Available

www.innerchildpress.com

Velvet Passions

of

Calibrated Quarks

Caroline Nazareno-Gabis

Now Available

www.innerchildpress.com

Unpaired

Eliza Segiet

Translated by Artur Komoter

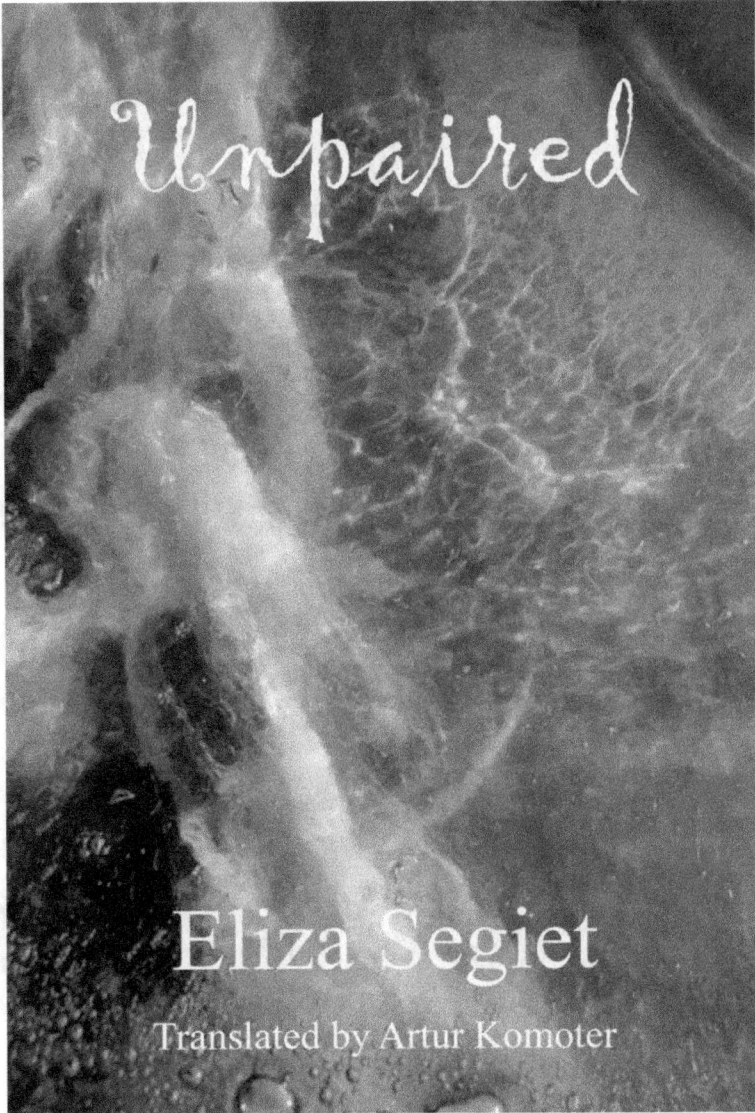

Private Issue

www.innerchildpress.com

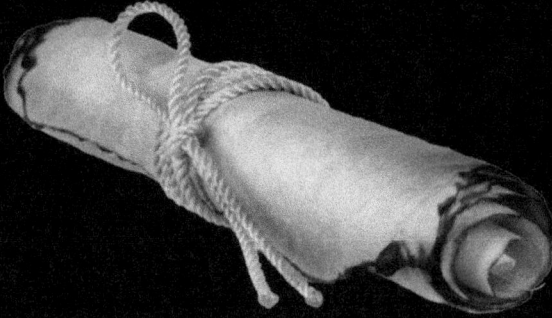

Canlarım

My Lifeblood

poetry in Turkish and English

hülya n. yılmaz

Now Available

www.innerchildpress.com

Butterfly's Voice

Faleeha Hassan

Translated by William M. Hutchins

Now Available at

www.innerchildpress.com

No Illusions

Through the Looking Glass

Jackie Davis Allen

Now Available at

www.innerchildpress.com

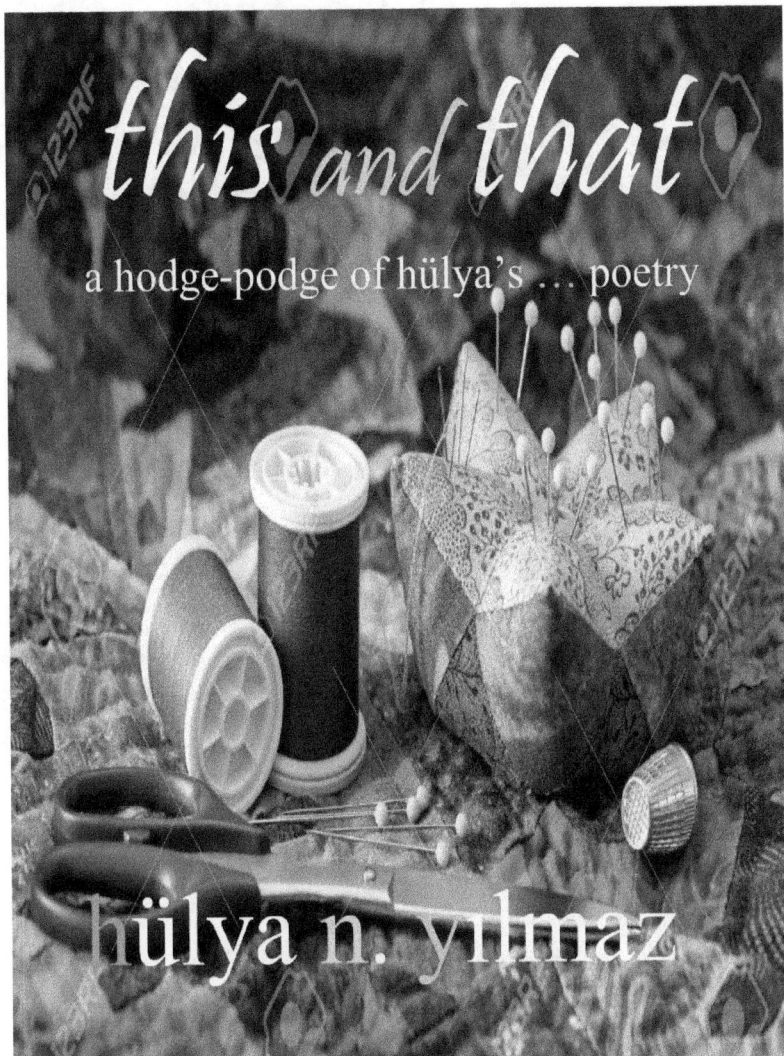

this and that
a hodge-podge of hülya's ... poetry

hülya n. yilmaz

Now Available at
www.innerchildpress.com

Eclectic Verse

mommy i hear those whispers . . . (again)

WilliAM s. PeTers, sR

Now Available at

www.innerchildpress.com

HERENOW

FAHREDIN SHEHU

Now Available at
www.innerchildpress.com

Magnetic People

Eliza Segiet

Translated by Artur Komoter

Now Available at

www.innerchildpress.com

Dark Side
of the
Moon

Jackie Davis Allen

Now Available at
www.innerchildpress.com

Lies My Grandfathers Told Me

Gail Weston Shazor

Now Available at
www.innerchildpress.com

Aflame

Memoirs in Verse

hülya n. yılmaz

Now Available at
www.innerchildpress.com

Mass Graves

Faleeha Hassan

Now Available at
www.innerchildpress.com

174

Breakfast

for

Butterflies

Faleeha Hassan

Now Available at

www.innerchildpress.com

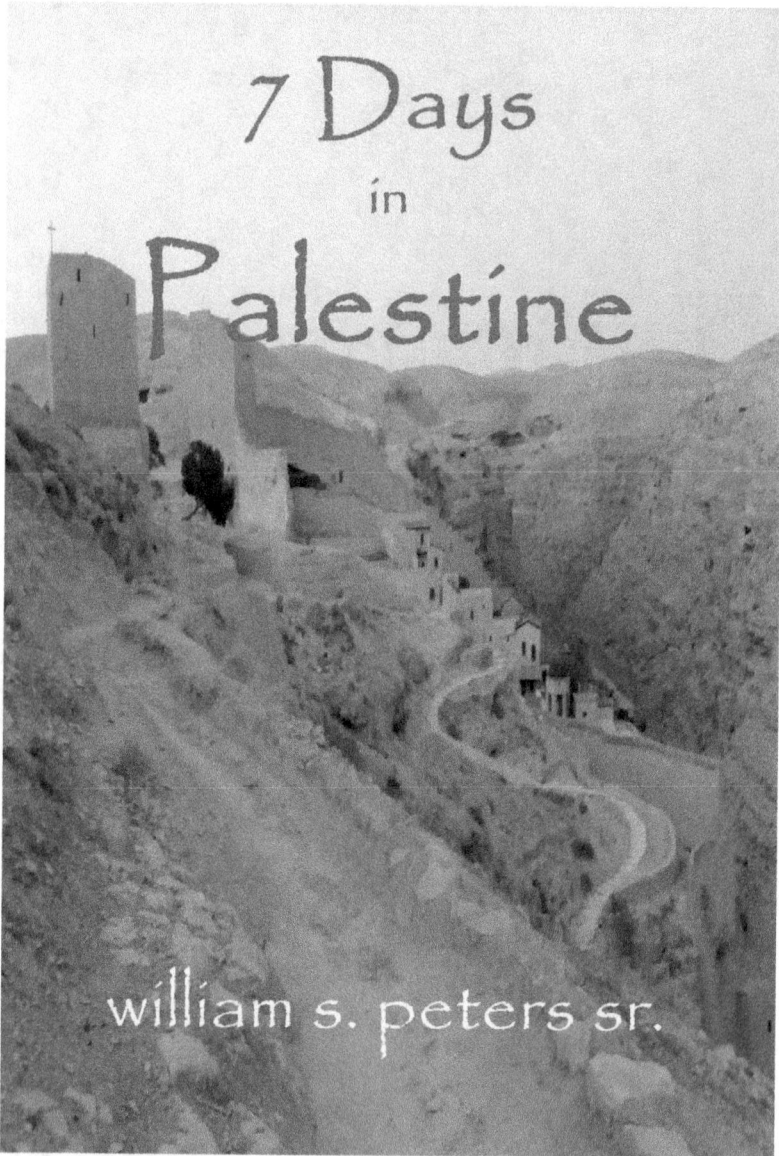

7 Days
in
Palestine

william s. peters sr.

Now Available at
www.innerchildpress.com

inner child press
presents

Tunisian Dreams

william s. peters, sr.

Now Available at

www.innerchildpress.com

INNER CHILD PRESS

THIS IS WHY I
SLEEP

william s. peters sr.

Now Available at
www.innerchildpress.com

Other

Anthological

works from

Inner Child Press International

www.innerchildpress.com

World Healing
World Peace
2022

Poets for Humanity

Now Available

www.worldhealingworldpeacepoetry.com

World Healing World Peace
2020

Poets for Humanity

Now Available

www.worldhealingworldpeacepoetry.com

I want to LiVe

*an **examination** of Black & White issues*

POETRY

ANALYSES

STORIES

CREATIVE WRITING

CRITICAL ESSAYS

WRITERS FOR HUMANITY

Now Available

www.innerchildpress.com

Inner Child Press International
&
The Year of the Poet
present

Poetry
the best of 2020

Poets of the World

Now Available
www.innerchildpress.com

Inner Child Press International

presents

W.A.R.

We Are Revolution

Poets for Humanity

Now Available
www.innerchildpress.com

the Heart of a Poet

words for a better tomorrow

The Conscious Poets

Now Available

www.innerchildpress.com

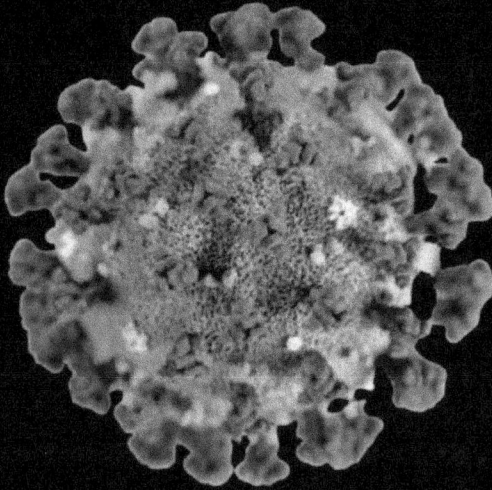

Corona

Social Distancing

Poets for Humanity

Now Available

www.innerchildpress.com

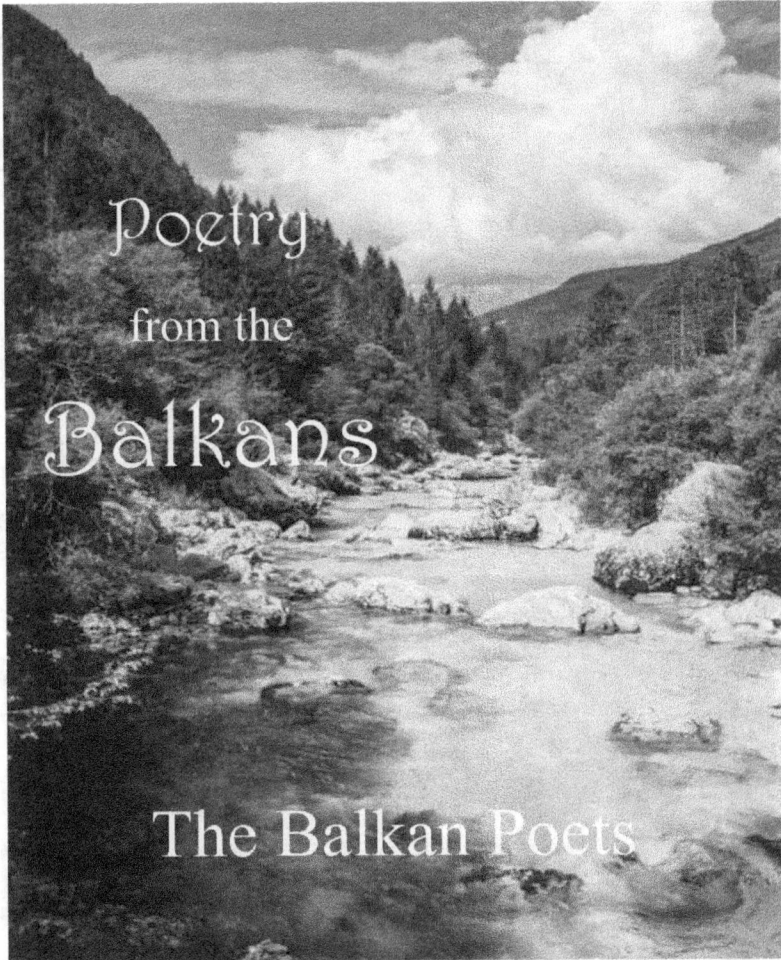

Poetry

from the

Balkans

The Balkan Poets

Now Available at

www.innerchildpress.com

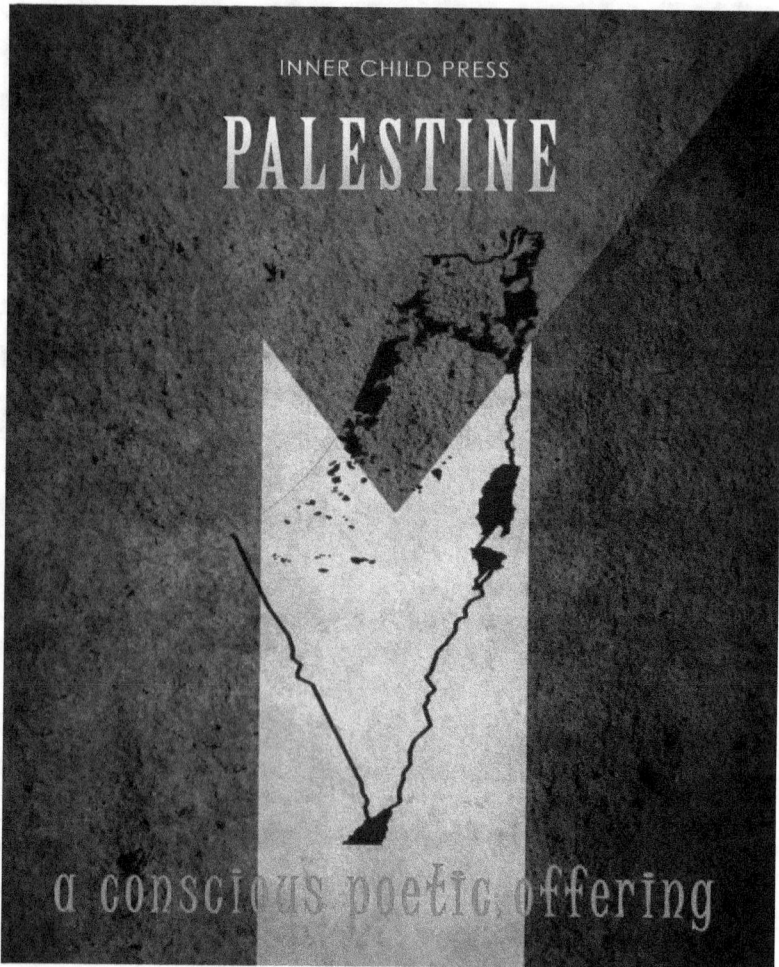

INNER CHILD PRESS

PALESTINE

a conscious poetic offering

Now Available at
www.innerchildpress.com

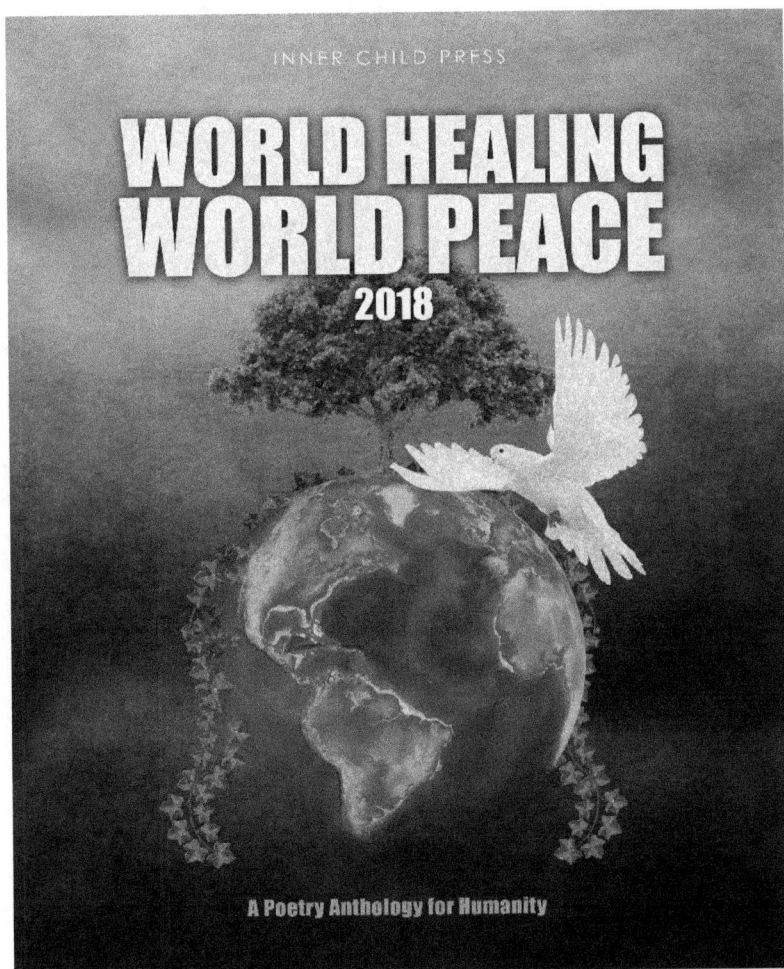

Now Available at

www.innerchildpress.com

Inner Child Press International
presents

A Love Anthology
2019

The Love Poets

Now Available

www.worldhealingworldpeacepoetry.com

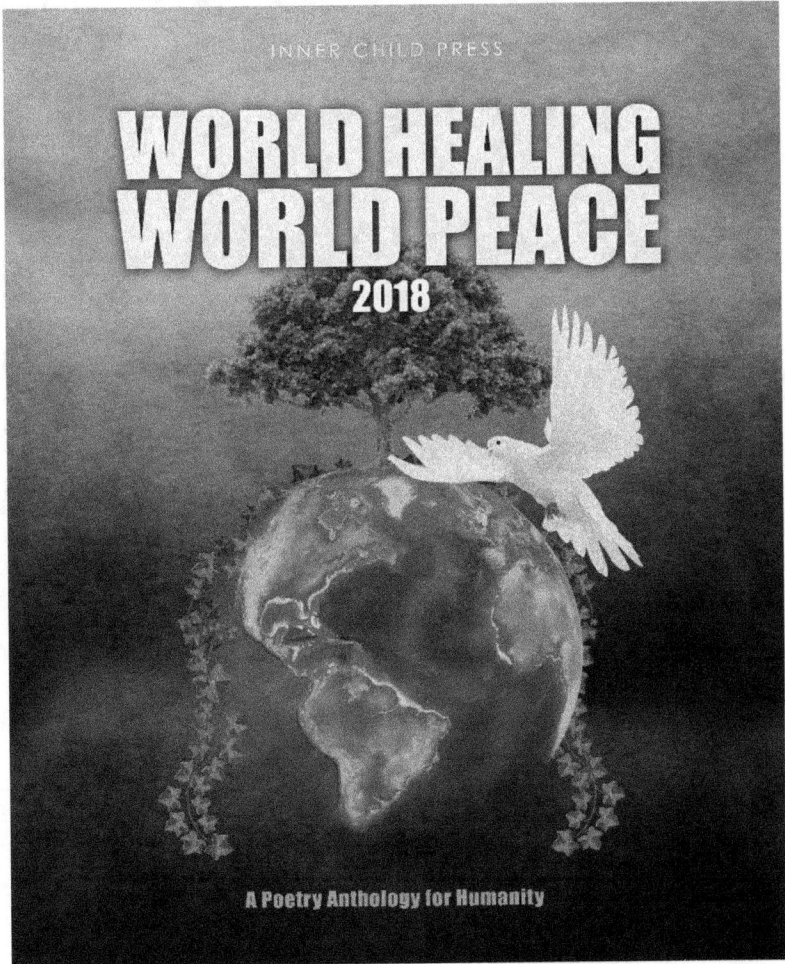

INNER CHILD PRESS

WORLD HEALING
WORLD PEACE
2018

A Poetry Anthology for Humanity

Now Available

www.worldhealingworldpeacepoetry.com

Now Available

www.worldhealingworldpeacepoetry.com

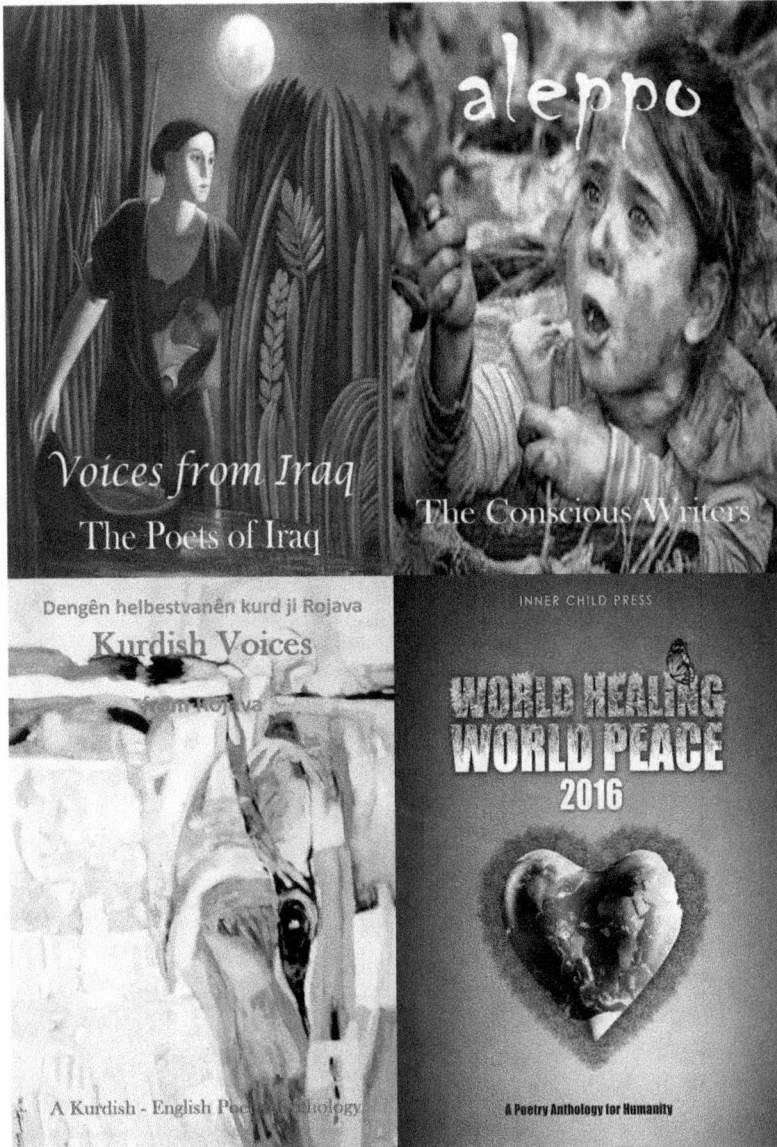

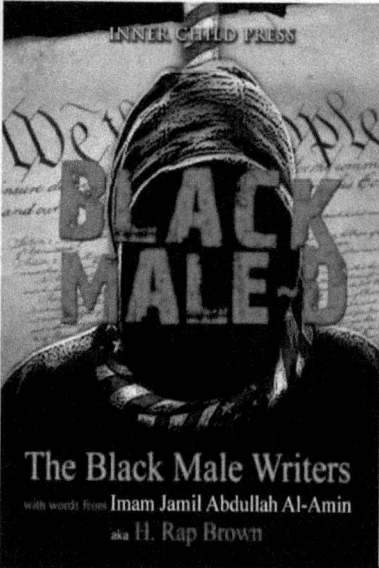

Now Available

Now Available

www.innerchildpress.com/anthologies

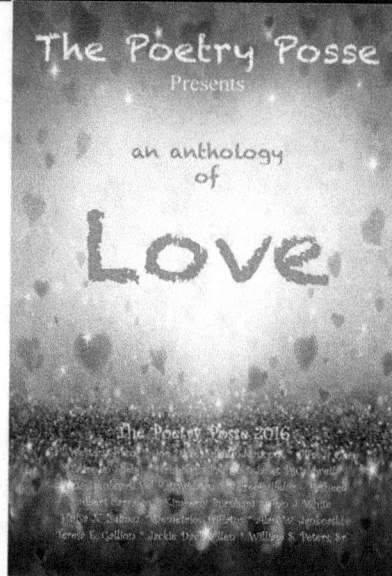

Now Available

www.innerchildpress.com/anthologies

Now Available

www.innerchildpress.com/anthologies

The Year of the Poet
January 2014

The Poetry Posse

Jamie Bond
Gail Weston Shazor
Albert 'Infinite' Carrasco
Siddartha Beth Pierce
Janet P. Caldwell
June 'Bugg' Barefield
Debbie M. Allen
Tony Henninger
Joe DaVerbal Minddancer
Robert Gibbons
Neetu Wali
Shareef Abdur-Rasheed
William S. Peters, Sr.

Carnation

Our January Feature

Terri L. Johnson

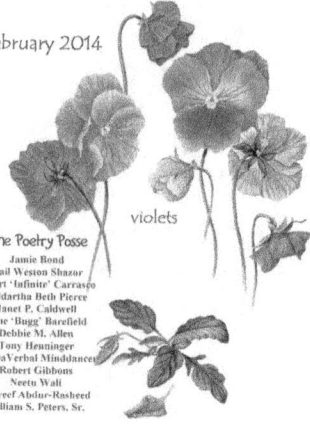

the Year of the Poet
February 2014

violets

The Poetry Posse

Jamie Bond
Gail Weston Shazor
Albert 'Infinite' Carrasco
Siddartha Beth Pierce
Janet P. Caldwell
June 'Bugg' Barefield
Debbie M. Allen
Tony Henninger
Joe DaVerbal Minddancer
Robert Gibbons
Neetu Wali
Shareef Abdur-Rasheed
William S. Peters, Sr.

Our February Features
Teresa E. Gallion & Robert Gibson

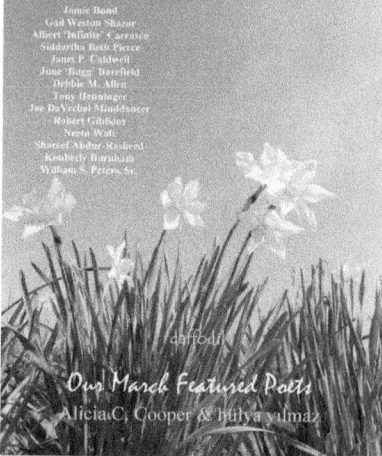

the Year of the Poet
March 2014

The Poetry Posse

Jamie Bond
Gail Weston Shazor
Albert 'Infinite' Carrasco
Siddartha Beth Pierce
Janet P. Caldwell
June 'Bugg' Barefield
Debbie M. Allen
Tony Henninger
Joe DaVerbal Minddancer
Robert Gibbons
Neetu Wali
Shareef Abdur-Rasheed
Kimberly Burnham
William S. Peters, Sr.

daffodil

Our March Featured Poets
Alicia C. Cooper & hülya yılmaz

the Year of the Poet
April 2014

The Poetry Posse

Jamie Bond
Gail Weston Shazor
Albert 'Infinite' Carrasco
Siddartha Beth Pierce
Janet P. Caldwell
June 'Bugg' Barefield
Debbie M. Allen
Tony Henninger
Joe DaVerbal Minddancer
Robert Gibbons
Neetu Wali
Shareef Abdur-Rasheed
Kimberly Burnham
William S. Peters, Sr.

Our April Featured Poets
Fahredin Shehu
Martina Reisz Newberry
Justin Blackburn
Monte Smith

Sweet Pea

celebrating international poetry month

Now Available
www.innerchildpress.com/the-year-of-the-poet

Now Available

www.innerchildpress.com/the-year-of-the-poet

The Year of the Poet

September 2014

Aster   Morning-Glory

Wild Cranium of Sister Hen Birthday Flower

September Feature Poets
Florence Malone * Keith Alan Hamilton

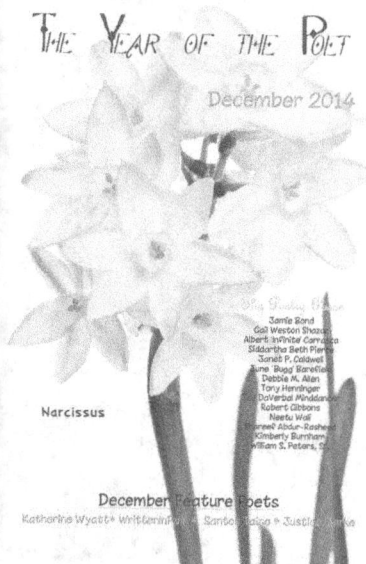

The Poetry Posse
Jamie Bond * Gail Weston Shazor * Albert 'Infinite' Carrasco * Siddartha Beth Pierce
Janet P. Caldwell * June 'Bugg' Barefield * Debbie M. Allen * Tony Henninger
Joe DaVerbal Minddancer * Robert Gibbons * Neetu Wali * Shareef Abdur-Rasheed
Kimberly Burnham * William S. Peters, Sr.

THE YEAR OF THE POET

October 2014

Red Poppy

The Poetry Posse
Jamie Bond * Gail Weston Shazor * Albert 'Infinite' Carrasco * Siddartha Beth Pierce
Janet P. Caldwell * June 'Bugg' Barefield * Debbie M. Allen * Tony Henninger
Joe DaVerbal Minddancer * Robert Gibbons * Neetu Wali * Shareef Abdur-Rasheed
Kimberly Burnham * William S. Peters, Sr.

October Feature Poets
Ceri Naz * Rajendra Padhi * Elizabeth Castillo

THE YEAR OF THE POET

November 2014

Chrysanthemum

The Poetry Posse
Jamie Bond * Gail Weston Shazor * Siddartha Beth Pierce
Janet P. Caldwell * June 'Bugg' Barefield * Debbie M. Allen * Tony Henninger
Joe DaVerbal Minddancer * Robert Gibbons * Neetu Wali * Shareef Abdur-Rasheed
Kimberly Burnham * William S. Peters, Sr.

November Feature Poets
Jocelyn Mosman * Jackie Allen * James Moore * Neville Hiatt

THE YEAR OF THE POET

December 2014

The Poetry Posse
Jamie Bond
Gail Weston Shazor
Albert 'Infinite' Carrasco
Siddartha Beth Pierce
Janet P. Caldwell
June 'Bugg' Barefield
Debbie M. Allen
Tony Henninger
DaVerbal Minddancer
Robert Gibbons
Neetu Wali
Shareef Abdur-Rasheed
Kimberly Burnham
William S. Peters, Sr.

Narcissus

December Feature Poets
Katherine Wyatt* Whitemanhawk* Santosh Bakaya * Justice Amina

Now Available

www.innerchildpress.com/the-year-of-the-poet

The Year of the Poet II
January 2015

Garnet

The Poetry Posse

Jamie Bond
Gail Weston Shazor
Albert 'Infinite' Carrasco
Siddartha Beth Pierce
Janet P. Caldwell
Tony Henninger
Joe DaVerbal Minddancer
Robert Gibbons
Neetu Wali
Shareef Abdur ~ Rasheed
Kimberly Burnham
Ann White
Keith Alan Hamilton
Katherine Wyatt
Fahredin Shehu
Hülya N. Yılmaz
Teresa E. Gallion
Jackie Allen
William S. Peters, Sr.

January Feature Poets
Bismay Mohanti ＊ Jen Walls ＊ Eric Judah

THE YEAR OF THE POET II
February 2015

Amethyst

THE POETRY POSSE

Jamie Bond
Gail Weston Shazor
Albert 'Infinite' Carrasco
Siddartha Beth Pierce
Janet P. Caldwell
Tony Henninger
Joe DaVerbal Minddancer
Robert Gibbons
Neetu Wali
Shareef Abdur ~ Rasheed
Kimberly Burnham
Ann White
Keith Alan Hamilton
Katherine Wyatt
Fahredin Shehu
Hülya N. Yılmaz
Teresa E. Gallion
Jackie Allen
William S. Peters, Sr.

FEBRUARY FEATURE POETS
Iram Fatima ＊ Bob McNeil ＊ Kerstin Centervall

The Year of the Poet II
March 2015

Our Featured Poets
Heung Sook ＊ Anthony Arnold ＊ Alicia Foland

Bloodstone

The Poetry Posse 2015
Jamie Bond * Gail Weston Shazor * Albert 'Infinite' Carrasco
Siddartha Beth Pierce * Janet P. Caldwell * Tony Henninger
Joe DaVerbal Minddancer * Neetu Wali * Shareef Abdur ~ Rasheed
Kimberly Burnham * Ann White * Keith Alan Hamilton
Katherine Wyatt * Fahredin Shehu * Hülya N. Yılmaz
Teresa E. Gallion * Jackie Allen * William S. Peters, Sr.

The Year of the Poet II
April 2015

Celebrating International Poetry Month

Our Featured Poets
Raja Williams ＊ Dennis Ferado ＊ Laure Charazac

Diamonds

The Poetry Posse 2015
Jamie Bond * Gail Weston Shazor * Albert 'Infinite' Carrasco
Siddartha Beth Pierce * Janet P. Caldwell * Tony Henninger
Joe DaVerbal Minddancer * Neetu Wali * Shareef Abdur ~ Rasheed
Kimberly Burnham * Ann White * Keith Alan Hamilton
Katherine Wyatt * Fahredin Shehu * Hülya N. Yılmaz
Teresa E. Gallion * Jackie Allen * William S. Peters, Sr.

Now Available

www.innerchildpress.com/the-year-of-the-poet

The Year of the Poet II
May 2015

May's Featured Poets

Geri Algeri
Akin Mosi Chinnery
Anna Jakubczak

Emeralds

The Poetry Posse 2015

Jamie Bond * Gail Weston Shazor * Albert 'Infinite' Carrasco
Siddartha Beth Pierce * Janet P. Caldwell * Tony Henninger
Joe DaVerbal Minddancer * Neetu Wali * Shareef Abdur – Rasheed
Kimberly Burnham * Ann White * Keith Alan Hamilton
Katherine Wyatt * Fahredin Shehu * Hülya N. Yılmaz
Teresa E. Gallion * Jackie Allen * William S. Peters, Sr.

The Year of the Poet II
June 2015

June's Featured Poets

Aashit Anastaanya * Yvette D. Murrell * Regina A. Walker

Pearl

The Poetry Posse 2015

Jamie Bond * Gail Weston Shazor * Albert 'Infinite' Carrasco
Siddartha Beth Pierce * Janet P. Caldwell * Tony Henninger
Joe DaVerbal Minddancer * Neetu Wali * Shareef Abdur – Rasheed
Kimberly Burnham * Ann White * Keith Alan Hamilton
Katherine Wyatt * Fahredin Shehu * Hülya N. Yılmaz
Teresa E. Gallion * Jackie Allen * William S. Peters. Sr

The Year of the Poet II
July 2015

The Featured Poets for July 2015
Abhik Shome * Christina Neal * Robert Neal

Rubies

The Poetry Posse 2015

Jamie Bond * Gail Weston Shazor * Albert 'Infinite' Carrasco
Siddartha Beth Pierce * Janet P. Caldwell * Tony Henninger
Joe DaVerbal Minddancer * Neetu Wali * Shareef Abdur – Rasheed
Kimberly Burnham * Ann White * Keith Alan Hamilton
Katherine Wyatt * Fahredin Shehu * Hülya N. Yılmaz
Teresa E. Gallion * Jackie Allen * William S. Peters. Sr.

The Year of the Poet II
August 2015

Peridot

Featured Poets
Gayle Howell
Ann Chalasz
Christopher Schultz

The Poetry Posse 2015

Jamie Bond * Gail Weston Shazor * Albert 'Infinite' Carrasco
Siddartha Beth Pierce * Janet P. Caldwell * Tony Henninger
Joe DaVerbal Minddancer * Neetu Wali * Shareef Abdur – Rasheed
Kimberly Burnham * Ann White * Keith Alan Hamilton
Katherine Wyatt * Fahredin Shehu * Hülya N. Yılmaz
Teresa E. Gallion * Jackie Allen * William S. Peters, Sr.

Now Available

www.innerchildpress.com/the-year-of-the-poet

The Year of the Poet II
September 2015

Featured Poets
Alfreda Ghee * Lonneice Weeks Badley * Demetrios Trifiatis

Sapphires

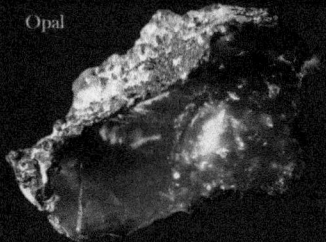

The Poetry Posse 2015
Jamie Bond * Gail Weston Shazor * Albert 'Infinite' Carrasco
Siddartha Beth Pierce * Janet P. Caldwell * Tony Henninger
Joe DaVerbal Minddancer * Neetu Wali * Shareef Abdur – Rasheed
Kimberly Burnham * Ann White * Keith Alan Hamilton
Katherine Wyatt * Fahredin Shehu * Hülya N. Yılmaz
Teresa E. Gallion * Jackie Allen * William S. Peters, Sr.

The Year of the Poet II
October 2015

Featured Poets
Monte Smith * Laura J Wolfe * William Washington

Opal

The Poetry Posse 2015
Jamie Bond * Gail Weston Shazor * Albert 'Infinite' Carrasco
Siddartha Beth Pierce * Janet P. Caldwell * Tony Henninger
Joe DaVerbal Minddancer * Neetu Wali * Shareef Abdur – Rasheed
Kimberly Burnham * Ann White * Keith Alan Hamilton
Katherine Wyatt * Fahredin Shehu * Hülya N. Yılmaz
Teresa E. Gallion * Jackie Allen * William S. Peters, Sr.

The Year of the Poet II
November 2015

Featured Poets
Alan W. Jankowski
Bismay Mohanty
James Moore

Topaz

The Poetry Posse 2015
Jamie Bond * Gail Weston Shazor * Albert 'Infinite' Carrasco
Siddartha Beth Pierce * Janet P. Caldwell * Tony Henninger
Joe DaVerbal Minddancer * Neetu Wali * Shareef Abdur – Rasheed
Kimberly Burnham * Ann White * Keith Alan Hamilton
Katherine Wyatt * Fahredin Shehu * Hülya N. Yılmaz
Teresa E. Gallion * Jackie Allen * William S. Peters, Sr.

The Year of the Poet II
December 2015

Featured Poets
Kerione Bryan * Michelle Joan Barulich * Neville Hiatt

Turquoise

The Poetry Posse 2015
Jamie Bond * Gail Weston Shazor * Albert 'Infinite' Carrasco
Siddartha Beth Pierce * Janet P. Caldwell * Tony Henninger
Joe DaVerbal Minddancer * Neetu Wali * Shareef Abdur – Rasheed
Kimberly Burnham * Ann White * Keith Alan Hamilton
Katherine Wyatt * Fahredin Shehu * Hülya N. Yılmaz
Teresa E. Gallion * Jackie Allen * William S. Peters, Sr.

Now Available

www.innerchildpress.com/the-year-of-the-poet

The Year of the Poet III

January 2016

Featured Poets

Lana Joseph * Atom Cyrus Rush * Christena Williams

Dark-eyed Junco

The Poetry Posse 2016

Gail Weston Shazor * Anne Jeucherek Vel Rettymsldon * Ann J. White
Dhrudin Shehu * Hrishikesh Padhye * Janet P. Caldwell
Joe DeVerbal Minddancer * Shareef Abdur - Rasheed
Albert Carrasco * Kimberly Burnham * Keith Alan Hamilton
Hulya N. Yilmaz * Demetrios Trifiatis * Alan W. Jankowski
Teresa E. Gallion * Jackie Davis Allen * William S. Peters, Sr.

The Year of the Poet III

February 2016

Featured Poets

Anthony Arnold
Anna Chalasz
DeAndre Hawthorne

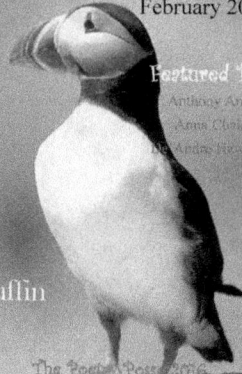

Puffin

The Poetry Posse 2016

Gail Weston Shazor * Joe DeVerbal Minddancer * Alfreda Ghee
Fahredin Shehu * Hrishikesh Padhye * Janet P. Caldwell
Anne Jakubczak, Vel Batty Adalan * Shareef Abdur - Rasheed
Albert Carrasco * Kimberly Burnham * Ann J. White
Hulya N. Yilmaz * Demetrios Trifiatis * Alan W. Jankowski
Teresa E. Gallion * Jackie Davis Allen * William S. Peters, Sr.

The Year of the Poet

March 2016

Featured Poets

Jeton Kelmendi   Nizar Sartawi   Sami Muhanna

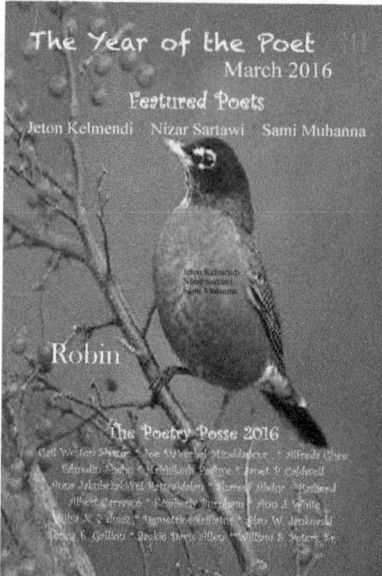

Jeton Kelmendi
Nizar Sartawi
Sami Muhanna

Robin

The Poetry Posse 2016

Gail Weston Shazor * Joe DeVerbal Minddancer * Alfreda Ghee
Fahredin Shehu * Hrishikesh Padhye * Janet P. Caldwell
Anne Jakubczak Vel Rettymsldon * Shareef Abdur - Rasheed
Albert Carrasco * Kimberly Burnham * Ann J. White
Hulya N. Yilmaz * Demetrios Trifiatis * Alan W. Jankowski
Teresa E. Gallion * Jackie Davis Allen * William S. Peters, Sr.

The Year of the Poet III

Featured Poets

Ali Abdolrezaei

Anna Chalasz

Agim Vinca

Ceri Naz

Black Capped Chickadee

The Poetry Posse 2016

Gail Weston Shazor * Joe DaVerbal Minddancer - * Alfreda Ghee
Fahredin Shehu * Hrishikesh Padhye * Janet P. Caldwell
Anna Jakubczak, Vel Ratty Adalan * Shareef Abdur - Rasheed
Albert Carrasco * Kimberly Burnham * Ann J. White
Hulya N. Yilmaz * Demetrios Trifiatis * Alan W. Jankowski
Teresa E. Gallion * Jackie Davis Allen * William S. Peters, Sr.

celebrating international poetry month

Now Available

www.innerchildpress.com/the-year-of-the-poet

The Year of the Poet III
May 2016

Bob Strum
Barbara Allan
D.L. Davis

Oriole

The Poetry Posse 2016

The Year of the Poet III
June 2016

Featured Poets

Qibrije Demiri- Frangu
Naime Beqiraj
Faleeha Hassan
Bedri Zyberaj

Black Necked Stilt

The Poetry Posse 2016

The Year of the Poet III
July 2016

Featured Poets

Iram Fatima 'Ashi'
Langley Shazor
Jody Doty
Emilia T. Davis

Indigo Bunting

The Poetry Posse 2016

The Year of the Poet III
August 2016

Featured Poets

Anita Dash
Irena Jovanovic
Malgorzata Gouluda

Painted Bunting

The Poetry Posse 2016

Now Available

www.innerchildpress.com/the-year-of-the-poet

The Year of the Poet III
September 2016

Featured Poets

Simone Weber
Abhijit Sen
Eunice Barbara C. Novio

Long Billed Curle

The Poetry Posse 2016

The Year of the Poet III
October 2016

Featured Poets

Luna Joseph
Uma Krishnamurthy
James Moore

Barn Owl

The Poetry Posse 2016

The Year of the Poet III
November 2016

Featured Poets

Rosemary Burns
Robin Ouzman Hislop
Lonneice Weeks-Badley

Northern Cardinal

The Poetry Posse 2016

The Year of the Poet III
December 2016

Featured Poets

Samih Masoud
Mountassir Aziz Bien
Abdulkadir Musa

Rough Legged Hawk

The Poetry Posse 2016

Now Available

www.innerchildpress.com/the-year-of-the-poet

The Year of the Poet IV
January 2017

Featured Poets

Jon Winell
Natalie Shields
Jumi Fatima "Ash"

Quaking Aspen

The Poetry Posse 2017

Gail Weston Shazor * Caroline Nazareno * Teresa Mehindy
Nizar Sartawi * Anna Jakubczak Vel Ratty Adalan * Jen Walls
Joe DaVerbal Minddancer * Shareef Abdur - Rasheed
Albert Carrasco * Kimberly Burnham * Elizabeth Castillo
Hülya N. Yılmaz * Fahreba Hassan * Alan W. Jankowski
Teresa E. Gallion * Jackie Davis Allen * William S. Peters, Sr.

The Year of the Poet IV
February 2017

Featured Poets

Lin Ross
Soukaina Fathi
Sraver Gitani

Witch Hazel

The Poetry Posse 2017

Gail Weston Shazor * Caroline Nazareno * Teresa Mehindy
Nizar Sartawi * Anna Jakubczak Vel Ratty Adalan * Jen Walls
Joe DaVerbal Minddancer * Shareef Abdur - Rasheed
Albert Carrasco * Kimberly Burnham * Elizabeth Castillo
Hülya N. Yılmaz * Fahreba Hassan * Alan W. Jankowski
Teresa E. Gallion * Jackie Davis Allen * William S. Peters, Sr.

The Year of the Poet IV
March 2017

Featured Poets

Tremell Stevens
Francisca Ricinski
Jamil Abu Shaih

The Eastern Redbud

The Poetry Posse 2017

Gail Weston Shazor * Caroline Nazareno * Teresa Mehindy
Teresa E. Gallion * Anna Jakubczak Vel Ratty Adalan
Joe DaVerbal Minddancer * Shareef Abdur - Rasheed
Albert Carrasco * Kimberly Burnham * Elizabeth Castillo
Hülya N. Yılmaz * Fahreba Hassan * Jackie Davis Allen
Jen Walls * Nizar Sartawi * * William S. Peters, Sr.

The Year of the Poet IV
April 2017

Featured Poets

Dr. Rachida Barman
Neptune Barman
Masoud Khalaf

The Blossoming Cherry

The Poetry Posse 2017

Gail Weston Shazor * Caroline Nazareno * Teresa Mehindy
Teresa E. Gallion * Anna Jakubczak Vel Ratty Adalan
Joe DaVerbal Minddancer * Shareef Abdur - Rasheed
Albert Carrasco * Kimberly Burnham * Elizabeth Castillo
Hülya N. Yılmaz * Fahreba Hassan * Jackie Davis Allen
Jen Walls * Nizar Sartawi * * William S. Peters, Sr.

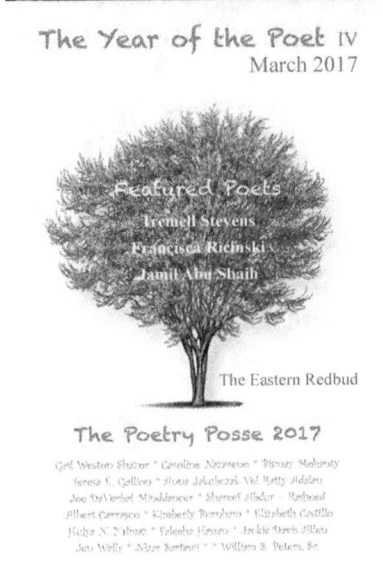

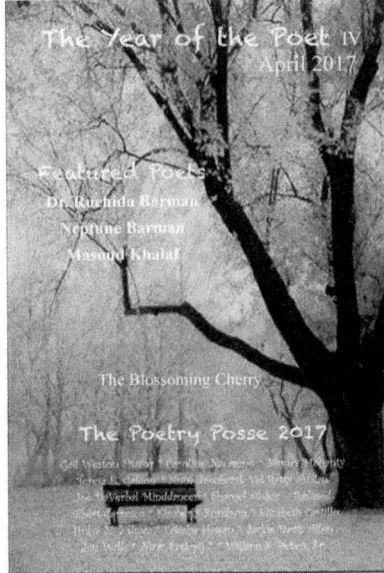

Now Available

www.innerchildpress.com/the-year-of-the-poet

The Year of the Poet IV
May 2017

The Flowering Dogwood Tree

Featured Poets
Kallisa Powell
Alicja Maria Kuberska
Fethi Sassi

The Poetry Posse 2017

The Year of the Poet IV
June 2017

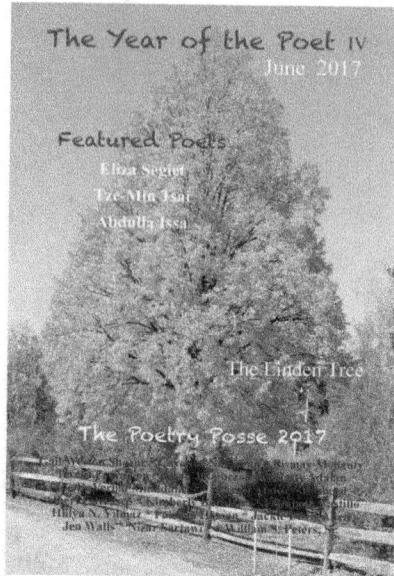

Featured Poets
Eliza Segiet
Tze-Min Tsai
Abdulla Issa

The Linden Tree

The Poetry Posse 2017

The Year of the Poet IV
July 2017

Featured Poets
Anca Mihaela Bruma
Ibaa Ismail
Zvonko Taneski

The Oak Moon

The Poetry Posse 2017

The Year of the Poet IV
August 2017

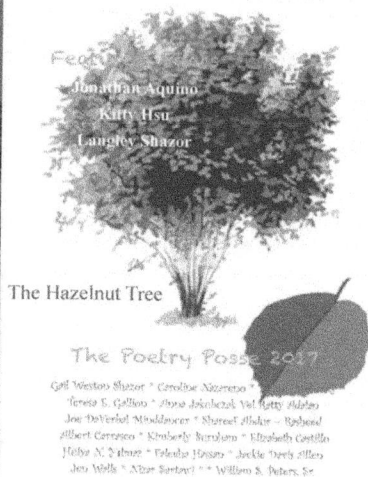

Featured Poets
Jonathan Aquino
Kitty Hsu
Langley Shazor

The Hazelnut Tree

The Poetry Posse 2017

Now Available
www.innerchildpress.com/the-year-of-the-poet

The Year of the Poet IV
September 2017

Featured Poets

Martina Reisz Newberry

Ameer Nassir

Christine Fulco Neal

Robert Neal

The Elm Tree

The Poetry Posse 2017

Gail Weston Shazor * Caroline Nazareno * Bismay Mohanty
Teresa E. Gallion * Anna Jakubczak Vel Ratty Adalan
Joe DaVerbal Minddancer * Shareef Abdur – Rasheed
Albert Carrasco * Kimberly Burnham * Elizabeth Castillo
Hülya N. Yılmaz * Faleeha Hassan * Jackie Davis Allen
Jen Walls * Nizar Sartawi * * William S. Peters, Sr.

The Year of the Poet IV
October 2017

Featured Poets

Ahmed Abu Saleem

Nedal Al-Qaeim

Sadeddin Shahin

The Black Walnut Tree

The Poetry Posse 2017

Gail Weston Shazor * Caroline Nazareno * Bismay Mohanty
Teresa E. Gallion * Anna Jakubczak Vel Ratty Adalan
Joe DaVerbal Minddancer * Shareef Abdur – Rasheed
Albert Carrasco * Kimberly Burnham * Elizabeth Castillo
Hülya N. Yılmaz * Faleeha Hassan * Jackie Davis Allen
Jen Walls * Nizar Sartawi * * William S. Peters, Sr.

The Year of the Poet IV
November 2017

Featured Poets

Kay Peters

Alfreda D. Ghee

Gabriella Garofalo

Rosemary Cappello

The Tree of Life

The Poetry Posse 2017

Gail Weston Shazor * Caroline Nazareno * Bismay Mohanty
Teresa E. Gallion * Anna Jakubczak Vel Ratty Adalan
Joe DaVerbal Minddancer * Shareef Abdur – Rasheed
Albert Carrasco * Kimberly Burnham * Elizabeth Castillo
Hülya N. Yılmaz * Faleeha Hassan * Jackie Davis Allen
Jen Walls * Nizar Sartawi * William S. Peters, Sr.

The Year of the Poet IV
December 2017

Featured Poets

Justice Clarke

Mariel M. Pabroa

Kiley Brown

The Fig Tree

The Poetry Posse 2017

Gail Weston Shazor * Caroline Nazareno * Bismay Mohanty
Teresa E. Gallion * Anna Jakubczak Vel Ratty Adalan
Joe DaVerbal Minddancer * Shareef Abdur – Rasheed
Albert Carrasco * Kimberly Burnham * Elizabeth Castillo
Hülya N. Yılmaz * Faleeha Hassan * William S. Peters, Sr.
Jen Walls * Nizar Sartawi * William S. Peters, Sr.

Now Available

www.innerchildpress.com/the-year-of-the-poet

The Year of the Poet V
January 2018
Featured Poets

Iyad Shamasnah

Yasmeen Hamzeh

Ali Abdolrezaei

Aksum

The Poetry Posse 2018
Gail Weston Shazor * Caroline Nazareno * Tezmin Ition Tsai
Hülya N. Yılmaz * Faleeha Hassan * Jackie Davis Allen
Teresa E. Gallion * Anna Jakubczak Vel Ratty Adalan
Alicja Maria Kubenska * Shareef Abdur – Rasheed
Kimberly Burnham * Elizabeth Castillo
Nizar Sartawi * William S. Peters, Sr.

The Year of the Poet V
February 2018

Sabean

Featured Poets

Muhammad Azram

Anna Szawracka

Abhilipsa Kuanar

Aanika Aery

The Poetry Posse 2018
Gail Weston Shazor * Caroline Nazareno * Tezmin Ition Tsai
Hülya N. Yılmaz * Faleeha Hassan * Jackie Davis Allen
Teresa E. Gallion * Anna Jakubczak Vel Ratty Adalan
Alicja Maria Kubenska * Shareef Abdur – Rasheed
Kimberly Burnham * Elizabeth Castillo
Nizar Sartawi * William S. Peters, Sr.

The Year of the Poet V
March 2018

Featured Poets

Iram Fatima 'Ashi'
Cassandra Swan
Jaleel Khazaal
Sharia Zaman

Mexico

Cuba

Dominican
Republic

Belize
Jamaica   Haiti
Guatemala   Puerto Rico
El Salvador   Honduras
Nicaragua
Costa Rica   Panama
Caribbean
&
Middle America
Colombia

The Poetry Posse 2018
Gail Weston Shazor * Nizar Sartawi * Hülya N. Yılmaz
Jackie Davis Allen * Caroline 'Ceri' Nazareno
Alicja Maria Kubenska * Teresa E. Gallion
Faleeha Hassan * Shareef Abdur – Rasheed
Kimberly Burnham * Elizabeth Castillo
Tezmin Ition Tsai * William S. Peters, Sr.

The Year of the Poet V
April 2018

Featured Poets

The Nez Perce

The Poetry Posse 2018

Now Available
www.innerchildpress.com/the-year-of-the-poet

The Year of the Poet V
May 2018

Featured Poets

Zaddy Carmen de León Jr
Sylwia K. Malinowska
Loulita Ahmeti
Olena Pisdon

The Sumerians

The Poetry Posse 2018

Gail Weston Shazor * Nizar Sartawi * Hülya N. Yılmaz
Jackie Davis Allen * Caroline 'Ceri' Nazareno
Alicja Maria Kuberska * Teresa E. Gallion
Kimberly Burnham * Shareef Abdur – Rasheed
Faleeha Hassan * Elizabeth Castillo * Swapna Behera
Tezmin Ition Tsai * William S. Peters, Sr.

The Year of the Poet V
June 2018

Featured Poets

Bilal Mahqi * Daim Miftari * Gojko Božović * Sofija Živković

The Paleo Indians

The Poetry Posse 2018

The Year of the Poet V
July 2018

Featured Poets

Tadiwed Dengue Daddy
Mohammad Ikbal Harb
Eliza Segiet
Tom Higgins

Oceania

The Poetry Posse 2018

Gail Weston Shazor * Nizar Sartawi * Hülya N. Yılmaz
Jackie Davis Allen * Caroline 'Ceri' Nazareno
Alicja Maria Kuberska * Teresa E Gallion
Kimberly Burnham * Shareef Abdur – Rasheed
Faleeha Hassan * Elizabeth Castillo * Swapna Behera
Tezmin Ition Tsai * William S. Peters, Sr.

The Year of the Poet V
August 2018

Featured Poets
Hussein Habasch * Mircea Dan Duta * Naida Mujkić * Swagat Das

The Lapita

The Poetry Posse 2018

Gail Weston Shazor * Nizar Sartawi * Hülya N. Yılmaz
Jackie Davis Allen * Caroline 'Ceri' Nazareno
Alicja Maria Kuberska * Teresa E. Gallion
Kimberly Burnham * Shareef Abdur – Rasheed
Ashok K. Bhargava* Elizabeth Castillo * Swapna Behaera
Tezmin Ition Tsai * William S. Peters, Sr

Now Available

www.innerchildpress.com/the-year-of-the-poet

The Year of the Poet V
September 2018

The Aztecs & Incas

Featured Poets
Kolade Olanrewaju Freedom
Elora Segar
Master Hussain Abdol Ghani
Lily Swarn

The Poetry Posse 2018

Gail Weston Shazor * Nizar Sartawi * Hülya N. Yılmaz
Jackie Davis Allen * Caroline 'Ceri' Nazareno
Alicja Maria Kubenska * Teresa E. Gallion
Kimberly Burnham * Shareef Abdur – Rasheed
Ashok K. Bhargava * Elizabeth Castillo * Swapna Behaera
Tezmin Ition Tsai * William S. Peters. Sr.

The Year of the Poet V
October 2018

Featured Poets
Alicia Minjarez * Lonneice Weeks-Hadley
Lopamudra Mishra * Abdelwahed Souayah

Bengali

The Poetry Posse 2018

Gail Weston Shazor * Nizar Sartawi * Hülya N. Yılmaz
Jackie Davis Allen * Caroline 'Ceri' Nazareno
Alicja Maria Kubenska * Teresa E. Gallion
Kimberly Burnham * Shareef Abdur – Rasheed
Ashok K. Bhargava * Elizabeth Castillo * Swapna Behaera
Tezmin Ition Tsai * William S. Peters. Sr.

The Year of the Poet V
November 2018

Featured Poets
Michelle Joan Barulich * Monsif Beroual
Krystyna Konecka * Nassira Nezzar

The Poetry Posse 2018

Gail Weston Shazor * Nizar Sartawi * Hülya N. Yılmaz
Jackie Davis Allen * Caroline 'Ceri' Nazareno
Alicja Maria Kubenska * Teresa E. Gallion
Kimberly Burnham * Shareef Abdur – Rasheed
Ashok K. Bhargava * Elizabeth Castillo * Swapna Behaera
Tezmin Ition Tsai * William S. Peters. Sr.

The Year of the Poet V
December 2018

Featured Poets
Rose Terranova Cirigliano
Joanna Kalinowska
Sokolović Emin
Dr. T. Ashok Chakravarthy

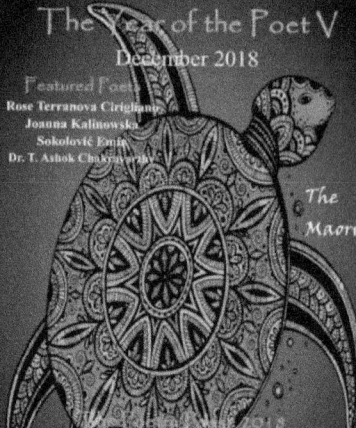

The Maori

The Poetry Posse 2018

Gail Weston Shazor * Nizar Sartawi * Hülya N. Yılmaz
Jackie Davis Allen * Caroline 'Ceri' Nazareno
Alicja Maria Kubenska * Teresa E. Gallion
Kimberly Burnham * Shareef Abdur – Rasheed
Ashok K. Bhargava * Elizabeth Castillo * Swapna Behera
Tezmin Ition Tsai * William S. Peters. Sr.

Now Available

www.innerchildpress.com/the-year-of-the-poet

The Year of the Poet VI

January 2019

Indigenous North Americans

Featured Poets

Houda Elfchtali
Anthony Briscoe
Iram Fatima 'Ashi'
Dr. K. K. Mathew

Dream Catcher

The Poetry Posse 2019

Gail Weston Shazor * Joe Paire * Hülya N. Yılmaz
Jackie Davis Allen * Caroline 'Ceri' Nazareno
Alicja Maria Kubeska * Teresa E. Gallion
Kimberly Burnham * Shareef Abdur - Rasheed
Ashok K. Bhargava * Elizabeth Castillo * Swapna Behera
Tezmin Ition Tsai * William S. Peters, Sr.

The Year of the Poet VI

February 2019

Featured Poets

Marek Łukaszewicz * Bharati Nayak
Aida G. Roque * Jean-Jacques Fournier

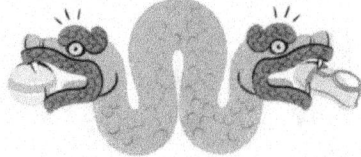

Meso-America

The Poetry Posse 2019

Gail Weston Shazor * Albert Carrasco * Hülya N. Yılmaz
Jackie Davis Allen * Caroline Nazareno * Eliza Segiet
Alicja Maria Kubeska * Teresa E. Gallion * Joe Paire
Kimberly Burnham * Shareef Abdur - Rasheed
Ashok K. Bhargava * Elizabeth Castillo * Swapna Behera
Tezmin Ition Tsai * William S. Peters, Sr.

The Year of the Poet VI

March 2019

Featured Poets

Enesa Mahmić * Sylwia K. Malinowska
Sharouk Hammoud * Anwer Ghani

The Caribbean

The Poetry Posse 2019

Gail Weston Shazor * Albert Carrasco * Hülya N. Yılmaz
Jackie Davis Allen * Caroline Nazareno * Eliza Segiet
Alicja Maria Kubeska * Teresa E. Gallion * Joe Paire
Kimberly Burnham * Shareef Abdur - Rasheed
Ashok K. Bhargava * Elizabeth Castillo * Swapna Behera
Tezmin Ition Tsai * William S. Peters, Sr.

The Year of the Poet VI

April 2019

Featured Poets

DL Davis * Michelle Joan Barulich
Lulëzim Haziri * Faleeha Hassan

Central & West Africa

The Poetry Posse 2019

Gail Weston Shazor * Albert Carrasco * Hülya N. Yılmaz
Jackie Davis Allen * Caroline Nazareno * Eliza Segiet
Alicja Maria Kubeska * Teresa E. Gallion * Joe Paire
Kimberly Burnham * Shareef Abdur - Rasheed
Ashok K. Bhargava * Elizabeth Castillo * Swapna Behera
Tezmin Ition Tsai * William S. Peters, Sr.

Now Available

www.innerchildpress.com/the-year-of-the-poet

The Year of the Poet VI

May 2019

Featured Poets

Emad Al-Haydary * Hussein Nasser Jabr
Wahab Sheriff * Abdul Razzaq Al Ameeri

Asia Southeast Asia and Maritime Asia

The Poetry Posse 2019

Gail Weston Shazor * Albert Carrasco * Hülya N. Yılmaz
Jackie Davis Allen * Caroline Nazareno * Eliza Segiet
Alicja Maria Kuberska * Teresa E. Gallion * Joe Paire
Kimberly Burnham * Shareef Abdur – Rasheed
Ashok K. Bhargava * Elizabeth Castillo * Swapna Behera
Tezmin Ition Tsai * William S. Peters, Sr.

The Year of the Poet VI

June 2019

Featured Poets

Kate Gaudi Powiekszone * Sahaj Sabharwal
Iwu Jeff * Mohamed Abdel Aziz Shmeis

Arctic
Circumpolar

The Poetry Posse 2019

Gail Weston Shazor * Albert Carrasco * Hülya N. Yılmaz
Jackie Davis Allen * Caroline Nazareno * Eliza Segiet
Alicja Maria Kuberska * Teresa E. Gallion * Joe Paire
Kimberly Burnham * Shareef Abdur – Rasheed
Ashok K. Bhargava * Elizabeth Castillo * Swapna Behera
Tezmin Ition Tsai * William S. Peters, Sr.

The Year of the Poet VI

July 2019

Featured Poets

Swaleddin Shaklo * Andy Scott
Fahredin Shehu * Alok Kumar Ray

The Horn of Africa

Ethiopia   Djibouti

Somalia   Eritrea

The Poetry Posse 2019

Gail Weston Shazor * Albert Carrasco * Hülya N. Yılmaz
Jackie Davis Allen * Caroline Nazareno * Eliza Segiet
Alicja Maria Kuberska * Teresa E. Gallion * Joe Paire
Kimberly Burnham * Shareef Abdur – Rasheed
Ashok K. Bhargava * Elizabeth Castillo * Swapna Behera
Tezmin Ition Tsai * William S. Peters, Sr.

The Year of the Poet VI

August 2019

Featured Poets

Shola Balogun * Bharati Nayak
Monalisa Dash Dwibedy * Mbizo Chirasha

Coexist

Southwest Asia

The Poetry Posse 2019

Gail Weston Shazor * Albert Carrasco * Hülya N. Yılmaz
Jackie Davis Allen * Caroline Nazareno * Eliza Segiet
Alicja Maria Kuberska * Teresa E. Gallion * Joe Paire
Kimberly Burnham * Shareef Abdur – Rasheed
Ashok K. Bhargava * Elizabeth Castillo * Swapna Behera
Tezmin Ition Tsai * William S. Peters, Sr.

Now Available

www.innerchildpress.com/the-year-of-the-poet

The Year of the Poet VI
September 2019

Featured Poets
Elena Liliana Popescu * Gobinda Biswas
Iram Fatima 'Ashi' * Joseph S. Spence, Sr.

The Caucasus

The Poetry Posse 2019

Gail Weston Shazor * Albert Carrasco * Hülya N. Yılmaz
Jackie Davis Allen * Caroline Nazareno * Eliza Segiet
Alicja Maria Kuberska * Teresa E. Gallion * Joe Paire
Kimberly Burnham * Shareef Abdur – Rasheed
Ashok K. Bhargava * Elizabeth Castillo * Swapna Behera
Tezmin Ition Tsai * William S. Peters, Sr.

The Year of the Poet VI
October 2019

Featured Poets
Ngozi Olivia Osuoha * Denisé Kondic
Pankhuri Sinha * Christena AV Williams

The Nile Valley

The Poetry Posse 2019

Gail Weston Shazor * Albert Carrasco * Hülya N. Yılmaz
Jackie Davis Allen * Caroline Nazareno * Eliza Segiet
Alicja Maria Kuberska * Teresa E. Gallion * Joe Paire
Kimberly Burnham * Shareef Abdur – Rasheed
Ashok K. Bhargava * Elizabeth Castillo * Swapna Behera
Tezmin Ition Tsai * William S. Peters, Sr.

The Year of the Poet VI
November 2019

Featured Poets
Ravaka Aleksandrova * Omoshu Ganga
Smruti Ranjan Mohanty * Sofia Skleida

Northern Asia

The Poetry Posse 2019

Gail Weston Shazor * Albert Carrasco * Hülya N. Yılmaz
Jackie Davis Allen * Caroline Nazareno * Eliza Segiet
Alicja Maria Kuberska * Teresa E. Gallion * Joe Paire
Kimberly Burnham * Shareef Abdur – Rasheed
Ashok K. Bhargava * Elizabeth Castillo * Swapna Behera
Tezmin Ition Tsai * William S. Peters, Sr.

The Year of the Poet VI
December 2019

Featured Poets
Kristin Kristic (Kristesse) * Irena Paul
Bharati Nayak * Kapardeli Eftichia

Oceania

The Poetry Posse 2019

Gail Weston Shazor * Albert Carrasco * Hülya N. Yılmaz
Jackie Davis Allen * Caroline Nazareno * Eliza Segiet
Alicja Maria Kuberska * Teresa E. Gallion * Joe Paire
Kimberly Burnham * Shareef Abdur – Rasheed
Ashok K. Bhargava * Elizabeth Castillo * Swapna Behera
Tezmin Ition Tsai * William S. Peters, Sr.

Now Available

www.innerchildpress.com/the-year-of-the-poet

The Year of the Poet VII

January 2020

Featured Poets

B S Tyagi * Ashok Chakravarthy Tholana
Andy Scott * Anwer Ghani

1901 Jean Henry Dunant and Frédéric Passy

The Year of Peace
Celebrating past Nobel Peace Prize Recipients

The Poetry Posse 2020

Gail Weston Shazor * Albert Carasco * Hülya N. Yılmaz
Jackie Davis Allen * Caroline Nazareno * Eliza Segiet
Alicja Maria Kuberska * Teresa E. Gallion * Joe Paire
Kimberly Burnham * Shareef Abdur – Rasheed
Ashok K. Bhargava * Elizabeth Castillo * Swapna Behera
Tezmin Ition Tsai * William S. Peters, Sr.

The Year of the Poet VII

February 2020

Featured Poets

Jennifer Ades * Martina Reisz Newberry
Ibrahim Honjo * Claudia Piccinno

Henri La Fontaine ~ 1913

The Year of Peace
Celebrating past Nobel Peace Prize Recipients

The Poetry Posse 2020

Gail Weston Shazor * Albert Carasco * Hülya N. Yılmaz
Jackie Davis Allen * Caroline Nazareno * Eliza Segiet
Alicja Maria Kuberska * Teresa E. Gallion * Joe Paire
Kimberly Burnham * Shareef Abdur – Rasheed
Ashok K. Bhargava * Elizabeth Castillo * Swapna Behera
Tezmin Ition Tsai * William S. Peters, Sr.

The Year of the Poet VII

March 2020

Featured Poets

Aziz Mountassir * Krishna Paraisa
Hannie Rouweler * Rozalia Aleksandrova

Aristide Briand ~ 1926 ~ Gustav Stresemann

The Year of Peace
Celebrating past Nobel Peace Prize Recipients

The Poetry Posse 2020

Gail Weston Shazor * Albert Carasco * Hülya N. Yılmaz
Jackie Davis Allen * Caroline Nazareno * Eliza Segiet
Alicja Maria Kuberska * Teresa E. Gallion * Joe Paire
Kimberly Burnham * Shareef Abdur – Rasheed
Ashok K. Bhargava * Elizabeth Castillo * Swapna Behera
Tezmin Ition Tsai * William S. Peters, Sr.

The Year of the Poet VII

April 2020

Featured Poets

Rohini Behera * Mircea Dan Duta
Monalisa Dash Dwibedy * NilavroNill Shoovro

Carlos Saavedra Lamas ~ 1936

The Year of Peace
Celebrating past Nobel Peace Prize Recipients

The Poetry Posse 2020

Gail Weston Shazor * Albert Carasco * Hülya N. Yılmaz
Jackie Davis Allen * Caroline Nazareno * Eliza Segiet
Alicja Maria Kuberska * Teresa E. Gallion * Joe Paire
Kimberly Burnham * Shareef Abdur – Rasheed
Ashok K. Bhargava * Elizabeth Castillo * Swapna Behera
Tezmin Ition Tsai * William S. Peters, Sr.

Now Available

www.innerchildpress.com/the-year-of-the-poet

The Year of the Poet VII
May 2020
Featured Poets
Alok Kumar Ray * Eden S. Trinidad
Franco Barbato * Izabela Zubko

Ralph Bunche ~ 1950

The Year of Peace
Celebrating past Nobel Peace Prize Recipients

The Poetry Posse 2020
Gail Weston Shazor * Albert Carasco * Hülya N. Yılmaz
Jackie Davis Allen * Caroline Nazareno * Eliza Segiet
Alicja Maria Kuberska * Teresa E. Gallion * Joe Paire
Kimberly Burnham * Shareef Abdur ~ Rasheed
Ashok K. Bhargava * Elizabeth Castillo * Swapna Behera
Tezmin Ition Tsai * William S. Peters, Sr.

The Year of the Poet VII
June 2020
Featured Poets
Eftichia Kapardeli * Metin Cengiz
Hussein Habasch * Kosh K Mathew

Albert John Lutuli ~ 1960

The Year of Peace
Celebrating past Nobel Peace Prize Recipients

The Poetry Posse 2020
Gail Weston Shazor * Albert Carasco * Hülya N. Yılmaz
Jackie Davis Allen * Caroline Nazareno * Eliza Segiet
Alicja Maria Kuberska * Teresa E. Gallion * Joe Paire
Kimberly Burnham * Shareef Abdur ~ Rasheed
Ashok K. Bhargava * Elizabeth Castillo * Swapna Behera
Tezmin Ition Tsai * William S. Peters, Sr.

The Year of the Poet VII
July 2020
Featured Poets
Mykola Martyniuk * Orbindu Ganga
Roula Pollard * Karn Praktisha

Norman Ernest Borlaug ~ 1970

The Year of Peace
Celebrating past Nobel Peace Prize Recipients

The Poetry Posse 2020
Gail Weston Shazor * Albert Carasco * Hülya N. Yılmaz
Jackie Davis Allen * Caroline Nazareno * Eliza Segiet
Alicja Maria Kuberska * Teresa E. Gallion * Joe Paire
Kimberly Burnham * Shareef Abdur ~ Rasheed
Ashok K. Bhargava * Elizabeth Castillo * Swapna Behera
Tezmin Ition Tsai * William S. Peters, Sr.

The Year of the Poet VII
August 2020
Featured Poets
Dr Pragya Suman * Chinh Nguyen
Srinivas Vasudev * Ugwu Leonard Ifeanyi, Jr.

Adolfo Pérez Esquivel ~ 1980

The Year of Peace
Celebrating past Nobel Peace Prize Recipients

The Poetry Posse 2020
Gail Weston Shazor * Albert Carasco * Hülya N. Yılmaz
Jackie Davis Allen * Caroline Nazareno * Eliza Segiet
Alicja Maria Kuberska * Teresa E. Gallion * Joe Paire
Kimberly Burnham * Shareef Abdur ~ Rasheed
Ashok K. Bhargava * Elizabeth Castillo * Swapna Behera
Tezmin Ition Tsai * William S. Peters, Sr.

Now Available

www.innerchildpress.com/the-year-of-the-poet

The Year of the Poet VII
September 2020
Featured Poets
Raed Anis Al Jishi • Sedkmeseré Snezana
Dr. Brajesh Kumar Gupta • Umid Nagari
Mikhail Sergeyevich Gorbachev ~ 1990

The Year of Peace
Celebrating past Nobel Peace Prize Recipients

The Poetry Posse 2020
Gail Weston Shazor • Albert Carasco • Hülya N. Yılmaz
Jackie Davis Allen • Caroline Nazareno • Eliza Segiet
Alicja Maria Kuberska • Teresa E. Gallion • Joe Paire
Kimberly Burnham • Shareef Abdur ~ Rasheed
Ashok K. Bhargava • Elizabeth Castillo • Swapna Behera
Tezmin Ition Tsai • William S. Peters, Sr

The Year of the Poet VII
October 2020
Featured Poets
Mutawaf A. Shaheed • Galina Italyanskaya
Nadeem Fraz • Avril Tanya Meallem
Kim Dae-jung ~ 2000

The Year of Peace
Celebrating past Nobel Peace Prize Recipients

The Poetry Posse 2020
Gail Weston Shazor • Albert Carasco • Hülya N. Yılmaz
Jackie Davis Allen • Caroline Nazareno • Eliza Segiet
Alicja Maria Kuberska • Teresa E. Gallion • Joe Paire
Kimberly Burnham • Shareef Abdur ~ Rasheed
Ashok K. Bhargava • Elizabeth Castillo • Swapna Behera
Tezmin Ition Tsai • William S. Peters, Sr

The Year of the Poet VII
November 2020
Featured Poets
Elisa Masera • Sue Lindenberg McClelland
Hatif Janabi • Ivan Gacina
Liu Xiaobo ~ 2010

The Year of Peace
Celebrating past Nobel Peace Prize Recipients

The Poetry Posse 2020
Gail Weston Shazor • Albert Carasco • Hülya N. Yılmaz
Jackie Davis Allen • Caroline Nazareno • Eliza Segiet
Alicja Maria Kuberska • Teresa E. Gallion • Joe Paire
Kimberly Burnham • Shareef Abdur ~ Rasheed
Ashok K. Bhargava • Elizabeth Castillo • Swapna Behera
Tezmin Ition Tsai • William S. Peters, Sr

The Year of the Poet VII
December 2020
Featured Poets
Ratan Ghosh • Ibtisam Ibrahim Al-Asady
Brindha Vinodh • Selma Kopic
Abiy Ahmed Ali ~ 2019

The Year of Peace
Celebrating past Nobel Peace Prize Recipients

The Poetry Posse 2020
Gail Weston Shazor • Albert Carasco • Hülya N. Yılmaz
Jackie Davis Allen • Caroline Nazareno • Eliza Segiet
Alicja Maria Kuberska • Teresa E. Gallion • Joe Paire
Kimberly Burnham • Shareef Abdur ~ Rasheed
Ashok K. Bhargava • Elizabeth Castillo • Swapna Behera
Tezmin Ition Tsai • William S. Peters, Sr.

Now Available

www.innerchildpress.com/the-year-of-the-poet

The Year of the Poet VIII

May 2021

Featured Global Poets

Paramita Mukherjee Mullick * Rose Zerguine
Jaydeep Sarangi * Bismay Mohanty

Diego Rivera

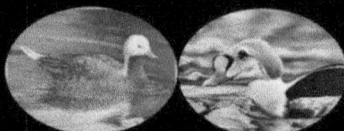

Poetry . . . Ekphrasticly Speaking

The Poetry Posse 2021

Gail Weston Shazor * Albert Carassco * Hülya N. Yılmaz
Jackie Davis Allen * Caroline Nazareno * Eliza Segiet
Alicja Maria Kuberska * Teresa E. Gallion * Joe Paire
Kimberly Burnham * Shareef Abdur – Rasheed
Ashok K. Bhargava * Elizabeth Castillo * Swapna Behera
Tezmin Ition Tsai * William S. Peters, Sr.

The Year of the Poet VIII

June 2021

Featured Global Poets

Alonzo "zO" Gross * Lali Tsipi Michaeli
Tareq al Karmy * Tirthendu Ganguly

Rayen Kang

Poetry . . . Ekphrasticly Speaking

The Poetry Posse 2021

Gail Weston Shazor * Albert Carassco * Hülya N. Yılmaz
Jackie Davis Allen * Caroline Nazareno * Eliza Segiet
Alicja Maria Kuberska * Teresa E. Gallion * Joe Paire
Kimberly Burnham * Shareef Abdur – Rasheed
Ashok K. Bhargava * Elizabeth Castillo * Swapna Behera
Tezmin Ition Tsai * William S. Peters, Sr.

The Year of the Poet VIII

July 2021

Featured Global Poets

Iram Jaan * Vesna Mundishevska-Veljanovska
Ngozi Olivia Osuoha * Lan Qyqalla

Goncalao Mabunda

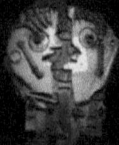

Poetry . . . Ekphrasticly Speaking

The Poetry Posse 2021

Gail Weston Shazor * Albert Carassco * Hülya N. Yılmaz
Jackie Davis Allen * Caroline Nazareno * Eliza Segiet
Alicja Maria Kuberska * Teresa E. Gallion * Joe Paire
Kimberly Burnham * Shareef Abdur – Rasheed
Ashok K. Bhargava * Elizabeth Castillo * Swapna Behera
Tezmin Ition Tsai * William S. Peters, Sr.

The Year of the Poet VIII

August 2021

Featured Global Poets

Caroline Laurent Turunc * Kamal Dhungana
Pankhuri Sinha * Paramita Mukherjee Mullick

Mundara Koorang

Poetry . . . Ekphrasticly Speaking

The Poetry Posse 2021

Gail Weston Shazor * Albert Carassco * Hülya N. Yılmaz
Jackie Davis Allen * Caroline Nazareno * Eliza Segiet
Alicja Maria Kuberska * Teresa E. Gallion * Joe Paire
Kimberly Burnham * Shareef Abdur – Rasheed
Ashok K. Bhargava * Elizabeth Castillo * Swapna Behera
Tezmin Ition Tsai * William S. Peters, Sr.

Now Available

www.innerchildpress.com/the-year-of-the-poet

The Year of the Poet VIII
September 2021
Featured Global Poets
Monsif Beroual * Sandesh Ghimire

Sharmila Poudel * Pavol Janik

Heather Jansch

Poetry . . . Ekphrasticly Speaking

The Poetry Posse 2021
Gail Weston Shazor * Albert Carasco * Hülya N. Yılmaz
Jackie Davis Allen * Caroline Nazareno * Eliza Segiet
Alicja Maria Kubenska * Teresa E. Gallion * Joe Paire
Kimberly Burnham * Shareef Abdur – Rasheed
Ashok K. Bhargava * Elizabeth Castillo * Swapna Behera
Tezmin Ition Tsai * William S. Peters, Sr.

The Year of the Poet VIII
October 2021
Featured Global Poets
C. E. Shy * Saswata Ganguly
Suranjit Gain * Hasiba Hilal

Dale Lamphere

Poetry . . . Ekphrasticly Speaking

The Poetry Posse 2021
Gail Weston Shazor * Albert Carasco * Hülya N. Yılmaz
Jackie Davis Allen * Caroline Nazareno * Eliza Segiet
Alicja Maria Kubenska * Teresa E. Gallion * Joe Paire
Kimberly Burnham * Shareef Abdur – Rasheed
Ashok K. Bhargava * Elizabeth Castillo * Swapna Behera
Tezmin Ition Tsai * William S. Peters, Sr.

The Year of the Poet VIII
November 2021
Featured Global Poets
Errol D. Bean * Ibrahim Honjo
Tanja Ajtic * Rajashree Mohapatra

Andy Goldsworthy

Poetry . . . Ekphrasticly Speaking

The Poetry Posse 2021
Gail Weston Shazor * Albert Carasco * Hülya N. Yılmaz
Jackie Davis Allen * Caroline Nazareno * Eliza Segiet
Alicja Maria Kubenska * Teresa E. Gallion * Joe Paire
Kimberly Burnham * Shareef Abdur – Rasheed
Ashok K. Bhargava * Elizabeth Castillo * Swapna Behera
Tezmin Ition Tsai * William S. Peters, Sr.

The Year of the Poet VIII
December 2021
Featured Global Poets
Orbinda Ganga * Fadairo Tesleem
Anthony Arnold * Iyad Shamasnah

Fredric Edwin Church

Poetry . . . Ekphrasticly Speaking

The Poetry Posse 2021
Gail Weston Shazor * Albert Carasco * Hülya N. Yılmaz
Jackie Davis Allen * Caroline Nazareno * Eliza Segiet
Alicja Maria Kubenska * Teresa E. Gallion * Joe Paire
Kimberly Burnham * Shareef Abdur – Rasheed
Ashok K. Bhargava * Elizabeth Castillo * Swapna Behera
Tezmin Ition Tsai * William S. Peters, Sr.

Now Available

www.innerchildpress.com/the-year-of-the-poet

The Year of the Poet IX
January 2022
Featured Global Poets
Ratan Ghosh * Christine Neil-Wright
Andrew Scott * Ashok Kumar

Climate Change : The Ice Cap

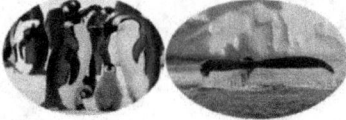

Poetry . . . Ekphrasticly Speaking

The Poetry Posse 2021

Gail Weston Shazor * Albert Carasco * Hülya N. Yılmaz
Jackie Davis Allen * Caroline Nazareno * Eliza Segiet
Alicja Maria Kuberska * Teresa E. Gallion * Joe Paire
Kimberly Burnham * Shareef Abdur – Rasheed
Ashok K. Bhargava * Elizabeth Castillo * Swapna Behera
Tezmin Ition Tsai * William S. Peters, Sr.

The Year of the Poet IX
February 2022
Featured Global Poets
Roza Boyanova * Ramón de Jesús Núñez Duval
Mammad Ismayil * Tarana Turan Rahimli

Climate Change and Mountains

Poetry . . . Ekphrasticly Speaking

The Poetry Posse 2021

Gail Weston Shazor * Albert Carasco * Hülya N. Yılmaz
Jackie Davis Allen * Caroline Nazareno * Eliza Segiet
Alicja Maria Kuberska * Teresa E. Gallion * Joe Paire
Kimberly Burnham * Shareef Abdur – Rasheed
Ashok K. Bhargava * Elizabeth Castillo * Swapna Behera
Tezmin Ition Tsai * William S. Peters, Sr.

The Year of the Poet IX
March 2022
Featured Global Poets
Dimitris P. Kraniotis * Marlene Pasini
Kennedy Ochieng * Swayam Prashant

Climate Change and Space Debris

Poetry . . . Ekphrasticly Speaking

The Poetry Posse 2021

Gail Weston Shazor * Albert Carasco * Hülya N. Yılmaz
Jackie Davis Allen * Caroline Nazareno * Eliza Segiet
Alicja Maria Kuberska * Teresa E. Gallion * Joe Paire
Kimberly Burnham * Shareef Abdur – Rasheed
Ashok K. Bhargava * Elizabeth Castillo * Swapna Behera
Tezmin Ition Tsai * William S. Peters, Sr.

The Year of the Poet IX
April 2022
Featured Global Poets
Alonzo Gross * Dr. Debaprasanna Biswas
Monsif Beroual * Carol Aronoff

Climate Change and Oceans

*Celebrating our 100th Edition *

Poetry . . . Ekphrasticly Speaking

The Poetry Posse 2021

Gail Weston Shazor * Albert Carasco * Hülya N. Yılmaz
Jackie Davis Allen * Caroline Nazareno * Eliza Segiet
Alicja Maria Kuberska * Teresa E. Gallion * Joe Paire
Kimberly Burnham * Shareef Abdur – Rasheed
Ashok K. Bhargava * Elizabeth Castillo * Swapna Behera
Tezmin Ition Tsai * William S. Peters, Sr.

Now Available

www.innerchildpress.com/the-year-of-the-poet

The Year of the Poet IX
May 2022

Featured Global Poets

Ndaba Sibanda * Smrutiranjan Mohanty
Ajanta Paul * Monalisa Dash Dwibedy

Climate Change and Birds

Poetry . . . Ekphrasticly Speaking

The Poetry Posse 2021

Gail Weston Shazor * Albert Carasco * Hülya N. Yılmaz
Jackie Davis Allen * Caroline Nazareno * Eliza Segiet
Alicja Maria Kuberska * Teresa E. Gallion * Joe Paire
Kimberly Burnham * Shareef Abdur – Rasheed
Ashok K. Bhargava * Elizabeth Castillo * Swapna Behera
Tezmin Ition Tsai * William S. Peters, Sr.

The Year of the Poet IX
June 2022

Featured Global Poets

Yuan Changming * Azeezat Okunlola
Tanja Ajtić * Philip Chijioke Abonyi

Climate Change and Trees

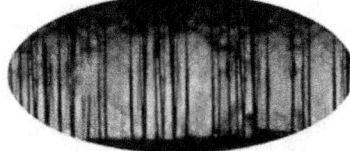

Poetry . . . Ekphrasticly Speaking

The Poetry Posse 2022

Gail Weston Shazor * Albert Carasco * Hülya N. Yılmaz
Jackie Davis Allen * Caroline Nazareno * Eliza Segiet
Alicja Maria Kuberska * Teresa E. Gallion * Joe Paire
Kimberly Burnham * Shareef Abdur – Rasheed
Ashok K. Bhargava * Elizabeth Castillo * Swapna Behera
Tezmin Ition Tsai * William S. Peters, Sr.

The Year of the Poet IX
July 2022

Featured Global Poets

Michelle Joan Barulich * Mili Das
Anna Ferriero * Ujjal Mandal

Climate Change and Animals

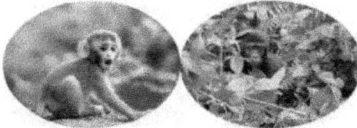

Poetry . . . Ekphrasticly Speaking

The Poetry Posse 2022

Gail Weston Shazor * Albert Carasco * Hülya N. Yılmaz
Jackie Davis Allen * Caroline Nazareno * Eliza Segiet
Alicja Maria Kuberska * Teresa E. Gallion * Joe Paire
Kimberly Burnham * Shareef Abdur – Rasheed
Ashok K. Bhargava * Elizabeth Castillo * Swapna Behera
Tezmin Ition Tsai * William S. Peters, Sr.

The Year of the Poet IX
August 2022

Featured Global Poets

Pankhuri Sinha * Abdulloh Abdumominov
Caroline Turunç * Tali Cohen Shabtai

Climate Change and Agriculture

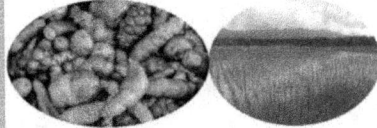

Poetry . . . Ekphrasticly Speaking

The Poetry Posse 2022

Gail Weston Shazor * Albert Carasco * Hülya N. Yılmaz
Jackie Davis Allen * Caroline Nazareno * Eliza Segiet
Alicja Maria Kuberska * Teresa E. Gallion * Joe Paire
Kimberly Burnham * Shareef Abdur – Rasheed
Ashok K. Bhargava * Elizabeth Castillo * Swapna Behera
Tezmin Ition Tsai * William S. Peters, Sr.

Now Available

www.innerchildpress.com/the-year-of-the-poet

The Year of the Poet IX
September 2022

Featured Global Poets

Ngozi Olivia Osuoha * Biswajit Mishra
Sylwia K. Malinowska * Sajid Hussein

Climate Change and Wind and Weather Patterns

Poetry . . . Ekphrasticly Speaking

The Poetry Posse 2022

Gail Weston Shazor * Albert Carasco * Hülya N. Yılmaz
Jackie Davis Allen * Caroline Nazareno * Eliza Segiet
Alicja Maria Kuberska * Teresa E. Gallion * Joe Paire
Kimberly Burnham * Shareef Abdur – Rasheed
Ashok K. Bhargava * Elizabeth Castillo * Swapna Behera
Tezmin Ition Tsai * William S. Peters, Sr.

The Year of the Poet IX
October 2022

Featured Global Poets

Andrew Kouroupos * Brenda Mohammed
Carthornia Kouroupos * Faleeha Hassan

Climate Change and Oil and Power

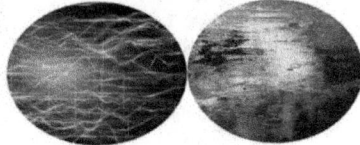

Poetry . . . Ekphrasticly Speaking

The Poetry Posse 2022

Gail Weston Shazor * Albert Carasco * Hülya N. Yılmaz
Jackie Davis Allen * Caroline Nazareno * Eliza Segiet
Alicja Maria Kuberska * Teresa E. Gallion * Joe Paire
Kimberly Burnham * Shareef Abdur – Rasheed
Ashok K. Bhargava * Elizabeth Castillo * Swapna Behera
Tezmin Ition Tsai * William S. Peters, Sr.

The Year of the Poet IX
November 2022

Featured Global Poets

Hema Ravi * Shafkat Aziz Hajam
Selma Kopic * Ibrahim Honjo

Climate Change : Time to Act

Poetry . . . Ekphrasticly Speaking

The Poetry Posse 2022

Gail Weston Shazor * Albert Carasco * Hülya N. Yılmaz
Jackie Davis Allen * Caroline Nazareno * Eliza Segiet
Alicja Maria Kuberska * Teresa E. Gallion * Joe Paire
Kimberly Burnham * Shareef Abdur – Rasheed
Ashok K. Bhargava * Elizabeth Castillo * Swapna Behera
Tezmin Ition Tsai * William S. Peters, Sr.

The Year of the Poet IX
December 2022

Featured Global Poets

Elarbi Abdelfattah * Lorraine Cragg
Neha Bhandarkar * Robert Gibbons

Climate Change Bees, Butterflies and Insect Life

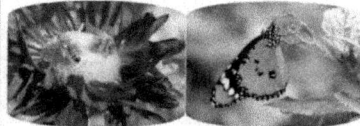

Poetry . . . Ekphrasticly Speaking

The Poetry Posse 2022

Gail Weston Shazor * Albert Carasco * Hülya N. Yılmaz
Jackie Davis Allen * Caroline Nazareno * Eliza Segiet
Alicja Maria Kuberska * Teresa E. Gallion * Joe Paire
Kimberly Burnham * Shareef Abdur – Rasheed
Ashok K. Bhargava * Elizabeth Castillo * Swapna Behera
Tezmin Ition Tsai * William S. Peters, Sr.

Now Available

www.innerchildpress.com/the-year-of-the-poet

The Year of the Poet X
January 2023
Featured Global Poets
JuNe Barefield * Swayam Prashant
Willow Rose * Shabbirhusein K Jamnagerwalla

Children - Difference Makers

Iqbal Masih

The Poetry Posse 2023

Gail Weston Shazor * Albert Carasco * Hülya N. Yilmaz
Jackie Davis Allen * Caroline Nazareno * Kimberly Burnham
Alicja Maria Kuberska * Teresa E. Gallion * Joe Paire
Michelle Joan Barulich * Shareef Abdur – Rasheed
Ashok K. Bhargava * Elizabeth Castillo * Swapna Behera
Tezmin Ition Tsai * Eliza Segiet * William S. Peters, Sr.

The Year of the Poet X
February 2023
Featured Global Poets
Christena Williams * Hilda Graciela Kraft
Francesco Favetta * Dr. H.C. Louise Hudon

Children - Difference Makers

Ruby Bridges

The Poetry Posse 2023

Gail Weston Shazor * Albert Carasco * Hülya N. Yilmaz
Jackie Davis Allen * Caroline Nazareno * Kimberly Burnham
Alicja Maria Kuberska * Teresa E. Gallion * Joe Paire
Michelle Joan Barulich * Shareef Abdur – Rasheed
Ashok K. Bhargava * Elizabeth Castillo * Swapna Behera
Tezmin Ition Tsai * Eliza Segiet * William S. Peters, Sr.

The Year of the Poet X
March 2023
Featured Global Poets
Clarena Martínez Turizo * Binod Dawadi
Til Kumari Sharma * Petrouchka Alexieva

Children - Difference Makers

Yo Yo Ma

The Poetry Posse 2023

Gail Weston Shazor * Albert Carasco * Hülya N. Yilmaz
Jackie Davis Allen * Caroline Nazareno * Kimberly Burnham
Alicja Maria Kuberska * Teresa E. Gallion * Joe Paire
Michelle Joan Barulich * Shareef Abdur – Rasheed
Ashok K. Bhargava * Elizabeth Castillo * Swapna Behera
Tezmin Ition Tsai * Eliza Segiet * William S. Peters, Sr.

The Year of the Poet X
April 2023
Featured Global Poets
Maxwanette A Poetess * Alonzo Gross
Türkan Ergör * Ibrahim Honjo

Children - Difference Makers

Claudette Colvin

The Poetry Posse 2023

Gail Weston Shazor * Albert Carasco * Hülya N. Yilmaz
Jackie Davis Allen * Caroline Nazareno * Kimberly Burnham
Alicja Maria Kuberska * Teresa E. Gallion * Joe Paire
Michelle Joan Barulich * Shareef Abdur – Rasheed
Ashok K. Bhargava * Elizabeth Castillo * Swapna Behera
Tezmin Ition Tsai * Eliza Segiet * William S. Peters, Sr.

Now Available

www.innerchildpress.com/the-year-of-the-poet

The Year of the Poet X
May 2023

Csp Shrivastava * Michael Lee Johnson
Taghrid Bou Merhi * Yasmin Brown

Children : Difference Makers

Louis Braille

The Poetry Posse 2023

Gail Weston Shazor * Albert Carasco * Hülya N. Yılmaz
Jackie Davis Allen * Caroline Nazareno * Kimberly Burnham
Alicja Maria Kuberska * Teresa E. Gallion * Joe Paire
Michelle Joan Barulich * Shareef Abdur – Rasheed
Ashok K. Bhargava * Elizabeth Castillo * Swapna Behera
Tezmin Ition Tsai * Eliza Segiet * William S. Peters, Sr.

The Year of the Poet X
June 2023

Featured Global Poets
Kay Peters * Carthornia Kouroupos
Andrew Kouroupos * Falecha Hassan

Children : Difference Makers

Ryan Hreljac

The Poetry Posse 2023

Gail Weston Shazor * Albert Carasco * Hülya N. Yılmaz
Jackie Davis Allen * Caroline Nazareno * Kimberly Burnham
Alicja Maria Kuberska * Teresa E. Gallion * Joe Paire
Michelle Joan Barulich * Shareef Abdur – Rasheed
Ashok K. Bhargava * Elizabeth Castillo * Swapna Behera
Tezmin Ition Tsai * Eliza Segiet * William S. Peters, Sr.

The Year of the Poet X
July 2023

Featured Global Poets
Rajashree Mohapatra * Biswajit Mishra
Johan Karlsson * Teodozja Świderska

Children : Difference Makers

~ Bana al-Abed ~

The Poetry Posse 2023

Gail Weston Shazor * Albert Carasco * Hülya N. Yılmaz
Jackie Davis Allen * Caroline Nazareno * Kimberly Burnham
Alicja Maria Kuberska * Teresa E. Gallion * Joe Paire
Michelle Joan Barulich * Shareef Abdur – Rasheed
Ashok K. Bhargava * Elizabeth Castillo * Swapna Behera
Tezmin Ition Tsai * Eliza Segiet * William S. Peters, Sr.

The Year of the Poet X
August 2023

Featured Global Poets
Kennedy Wanda Ochieng * Jose Lopez
Sylwia K. Malinowska * Laurent Grison

Children : Difference Makers

~ Kelvin Doe ~

The Poetry Posse 2023

Gail Weston Shazor * Albert Carasco * Hülya N. Yılmaz
Jackie Davis Allen * Caroline Nazareno * Kimberly Burnham
Alicja Maria Kuberska * Teresa E. Gallion * Joe Paire
Michelle Joan Barulich * Shareef Abdur – Rasheed
Ashok K. Bhargava * Elizabeth Castillo * Swapna Behera
Tezmin Ition Tsai * Eliza Segiet * William S. Peters, Sr.

Now Available

www.innerchildpress.com/the-year-of-the-poet

and there is much, much more !

visit . . .

www.innerchildpress.com/antho logies-sales-special.php

Also check out our Authors and all the wonderful Books Available at :

www.innerchildpress.com/autho rs-pages

World Healing World Peace
2020

Poets for Humanity

Now Available

www.worldhealingworldpeacepoetry.com

INNER CHILD PRESS

WORLD HEALING
WORLD PEACE
2018

A Poetry Anthology for Humanity

Now Available

www.worldhealingworldpeacepoetry.com

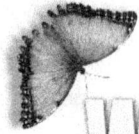

i support
World Healing
World Peace

www.worldhealingworldpeacepoetry.com

World Healing World Peace

World Healing
World Peace
2012, 2014, 2016, 2018, 2020, 2022

Now Available

www.worldhealingworldpeacepoetry.com

Inner Child Press International

'building bridges of cultural understanding'

Meet the Board of Directors

www.innerchildpress.com

Inner Child Press International

'building bridges of cultural understanding'

Meet our Cultural Ambassadors

Fahredin Shehu
Director of Cultural

Faleha Hassan
Iraq - USA

Elizabeth E. Castillo
Philippines

Antoinette Coleman
Chicago
Midwest USA

Ananshi Nejull
Nepal - Tibet
Northen Indy

Kimberly Burnham
Pacific Northwest
USA

Alicja Kuberska
Poland
Eastern Europe

Swapna Behera
India
Southeast Asia

Kolade O. Freedom
Nigeria
West Africa

Monsif Beroual
Morocco
Northern Afric

Ashok K. Bhargava
Canada

Tzemin Ition Tsai
Republic of China
Greater China

Alicia M. Ramírez
Mexico
Central America

Christena AV Williams
Jamaica
Caribbean

Louise Hudon
Eastern Canada

Aziz Mountassir
Morocco
Northern Africa

Sharef Abdur-Rasheed
Southeastern USA

Laure Charazac
France
Western Europe

Mohammad Ikbal Harb
Lebanon
Middle East

Mohamed Ahoof
Aziz Shmeh
Egypt
Middle East

Hilary Malnga
Congo
Eastern Africa

Josephus R. Johnson
Liberia

www.innerchildpress.com

This Anthological Publication
is underwritten solely by

Inner Child Press International

Inner Child Press is a Publishing Company
Founded and Operated by Writers. Our
personal publishing experiences provides
us an intimate understanding of the
sometimes daunting challenges Writers,
New and Seasoned may face in the
Business of Publishing and Marketing
their Creative "Written Work".

For more Information

Inner Child Press International

www.innerchildpress.com

'building bridges of cultural understanding'

202 Wiltree Court, State College, Pennsylvania 16801

www.innerchildpress.com

~ *fini* ~

www.ingramcontent.com/pod-product-compliance
Lightning Source LLC
LaVergne TN
LVHW022321080426
835508LV00041B/1680